Gun Violence

Opposing Viewpoints®

Other Books of Related Interest

Gun Violence

Opposing Viewpoints®

James D. Torr, *Book Editor*

Daniel Leone, *Publisher*
Bonnie Szumski, *Editorial Director*
Scott Barbour, *Managing Editor*

OPPOSING
VIEWPOINTS®
SERIES

Greenhaven Press, Inc., San Diego, California

Cover photo: Corbis Images, Inc.

Library of Congress Cataloging-in-Publication Data

Gun violence : opposing viewpoints / James D. Torr, book editor.
   p. cm. — (Opposing viewpoints series)
   Includes bibliographical references and index.
   ISBN 0-7377-0712-7 (pbk. : alk. paper) —
   ISBN 0-7377-0713-5 (lib. : alk. paper)
   1. Gun control—United States. 2. Violent crimes—United
States. 3. Firearms ownership—Government policy—United
States. I. Torr, James D., 1974–   II. Opposing viewpoints series
(Unnumbered)

HV7436 .G876 2002
363.3'3'0973—dc21   00-069172
                                                              CIP

Greenhaven Press, Inc., P.O. Box 289009
San Diego, CA 92198-9009

"Congress shall make no law...abridging the freedom of speech, or of the press."

First Amendment to the U.S. Constitution

The basic foundation of our democracy is the First Amendment guarantee of freedom of expression. The Opposing Viewpoints Series is dedicated to the concept of this basic freedom and the idea that it is more important to practice it than to enshrine it.

Contents

Why Consider Opposing Viewpoints?

"The only way in which a human being can make some approach to knowing the whole of a subject is by hearing what can be said about it by persons of every variety of opinion and studying all modes in which it can be looked at by every character of mind. No wise man ever acquired his wisdom in any mode but this."

John Stuart Mill

In our media-intensive culture it is not difficult to find differing opinions. Thousands of newspapers and magazines and dozens of radio and television talk shows resound with differing points of view. The difficulty lies in deciding which opinion to agree with and which "experts" seem the most credible. The more inundated we become with differing opinions and claims, the more essential it is to hone critical reading and thinking skills to evaluate these ideas. Opposing Viewpoints books address this problem directly by presenting stimulating debates that can be used to enhance and teach these skills. The varied opinions contained in each book examine many different aspects of a single issue. While examining these conveniently edited opposing views, readers can develop critical thinking skills such as the ability to compare and contrast authors' credibility, facts, argumentation styles, use of persuasive techniques, and other stylistic tools. In short, the Opposing Viewpoints Series is an ideal way to attain the higher-level thinking and reading skills so essential in a culture of diverse and contradictory opinions.

In addition to providing a tool for critical thinking, Opposing Viewpoints books challenge readers to question their own strongly held opinions and assumptions. Most people form their opinions on the basis of upbringing, peer pressure, and personal, cultural, or professional bias. By reading carefully balanced opposing views, readers must directly confront new ideas as well as the opinions of those with whom they disagree. This is not to simplistically argue that everyone who reads opposing views will—or should—change his or her opinion. Instead, the series enhances readers' understanding of their own views by encouraging confrontation with opposing ideas. Careful examination of others' views can lead to the readers' understanding of the logical inconsistencies in their own opinions, perspective on why they hold an opinion, and the consideration of the possibility that their opinion requires further evaluation.

Evaluating Other Opinions

To ensure that this type of examination occurs, Opposing Viewpoints books present all types of opinions. Prominent spokespeople on different sides of each issue as well as well-known professionals from many disciplines challenge the reader. An additional goal of the series is to provide a forum for other, less known, or even unpopular viewpoints. The opinion of an ordinary person who has had to make the decision to cut off life support from a terminally ill relative, for example, may be just as valuable and provide just as much insight as a medical ethicist's professional opinion. The editors have two additional purposes in including these less known views. One, the editors encourage readers to respect others' opinions—even when not enhanced by professional credibility. It is only by reading or listening to and objectively evaluating others' ideas that one can determine whether they are worthy of consideration. Two, the inclusion of such viewpoints encourages the important critical thinking skill of objectively evaluating an author's credentials and bias. This evaluation will illuminate an author's reasons for taking a particular stance on an issue and will aid in readers' evaluation of the author's ideas.

It is our hope that these books will give readers a deeper understanding of the issues debated and an appreciation of the complexity of even seemingly simple issues when good and honest people disagree. This awareness is particularly important in a democratic society such as ours in which people enter into public debate to determine the common good. Those with whom one disagrees should not be regarded as enemies but rather as people whose views deserve careful examination and may shed light on one's own.

Thomas Jefferson once said that "difference of opinion leads to inquiry, and inquiry to truth." Jefferson, a broadly educated man, argued that "if a nation expects to be ignorant and free . . . it expects what never was and never will be." As individuals and as a nation, it is imperative that we consider the opinions of others and examine them with skill and discernment. The Opposing Viewpoints Series is intended to help readers achieve this goal.

David L. Bender and Bruno Leone,
Founders

Greenhaven Press anthologies primarily consist of previously published material taken from a variety of sources, including periodicals, books, scholarly journals, newspapers, government documents, and position papers from private and public organizations. These original sources are often edited for length and to ensure their accessibility for a young adult audience. The anthology editors also change the original titles of these works in order to clearly present the main thesis of each viewpoint and to explicitly indicate the opinion presented in the viewpoint. These alterations are made in consideration of both the reading and comprehension levels of a young adult audience. Every effort is made to ensure that Greenhaven Press accurately reflects the original intent of the authors included in this anthology.

Introduction

"If there is one point in the gun control debate about which opponents are likely to agree, it is this: There is too much violent crime in the United States, and guns are too often involved in such crimes."

—*Earl R. Kruschke, author of*
Gun Control: A Reference Handbook

"The assassination of President John F. Kennedy in November 1963," write Jan E. Dizard, Robert Merril Muth, and Stephen P. Andrews Jr. in the introduction to *Guns in America: A Reader*, "set off a national debate over the place of firearms in our society that has continued, virtually unabated, to the present." Prior to Kennedy's death, firearms were commonly sold over-the-counter and through mail-order catalogs to almost any adult who wanted them. Then, in part because of the public outcry after Kennedy's assassination, Congress passed the Gun Control Act of 1968, which expanded gun-dealer licensing requirements and banned most felons, the mentally incompetent, and illegal drug users from buying guns. In signing the legislation, President Lyndon Johnson said, "Today we begin to disarm the criminal and the careless and the insane," but he lamented that the bill fell short because "we just could not get Congress to carry out the requests . . . for the national registration of all guns and the licensing of those who carry guns."

Historically, concern about gun violence has usually followed a high-profile shooting, as it did with the Kennedy assassination. On March 30, 1981, another such shooting occurred, this time a failed assassination attempt on President Ronald Reagan. The president and three others were wounded, and presidential press secretary James S. Brady was permanently disabled from his injuries. His wife Sarah subsequently became the head of Handgun Control Inc., the leading gun control advocacy group in the United States.

In the wake of the assassination attempt, gun control advocates pushed for tighter restrictions on gun sales. They argued that while the 1968 Gun Control Act banned gun sales to most criminals, it was still easy for criminals to lie to gun dealers about their identity or their past. A bill, named after James Brady, was introduced in Congress that would require background checks of all gun purchasers. Since the background checks could take several days, the bill also necessitated a waiting period on gun purchases.

The Brady Bill, however, faced considerable opposition from many congressmen, as well as President Reagan and his successor George Bush. The bill did not become law until 1993, after President Bill Clinton took office. The Clinton administration also instituted a ban on military-style "assault weapons" as part of its 1994 Omnibus Crime Bill. Since these two bills were passed, however, there has been no major gun legislation from the federal government.

This lack of federal government action is partly the result of Republican control of both the House and Senate since 1995. (Broadly speaking, Democrats tend to favor gun control legislation, while Republicans are generally resistant to stricter gun laws.) Many Republican legislators side with the National Rifle Association (NRA) on gun control issues. The NRA is the nation's largest organization of gun owners, and its members believe that gun control laws are unconstitutional and ineffective in reducing crime.

In the late 1990s, however, a series of school shootings, such as the one at Columbine High School in Littleton, Colorado, in which two heavily armed students killed 12 students and one teacher, shocked the nation and again renewed public debate over the availability of guns. Gun control advocates argued that many of the shootings could have been prevented if the students had not had such easy access to guns.

Gun rights advocates countered that responsible gun use sometimes saves lives. For example, the October 1997 incident in Pearl, Mississippi, in which a 17-year-old killed two students and wounded seven others at his high school, was brought to an end when the assistant principal of the school retrieved the pistol he kept in his car and subdued the shooter. Opponents of gun control also employed the classic logic of "guns don't kill people; people kill people," by arguing that in each of the school shootings, the killers were clearly disturbed and that the availability of guns wasn't the deciding factor that caused them to go on their rampages.

Policymakers, in the end, must confront the practical questions: What can be done to reduce the levels of gun violence in America? Does the problem of gun violence warrant further restrictions on gun ownership? There is a great divide on these basic questions. Groups like Handgun Control Inc. call for a total ban on handguns as well as licensing and registration of rifles and other so-called long guns. The National Rifle Association counters that guns are a vital means of self-defense, that gun ownership is a constitutional right, and, in another often-used phrase, that "when guns are outlawed, only criminals will have guns."

As Dizard, Muth, and Andrews note, the bitter nature of the debate between pro- and anti-gun groups often ends up leaving many Americans feeling more distraught about the problem of gun violence:

> Both pro-gun and anti-gun forces promote a sense of precariousness. The pro-gun folks portray a nation on the verge of anarchy that requires law-abiding people to arm themselves in self-defense. The anti-gun folks portray a nation awash in guns, held hostage to the impulsive acts of unstable people. . . . Paradoxically, the pro- and anti-gun extremists feed each other's fears. The consequences of this not only harden the opposition but also help to reinforce the pervasive sense of danger that grips so many Americans.

The viewpoints in *Gun Violence: Opposing Viewpoints* represent both moderate and extreme positions on issues of gun ownership, gun control, and violence prevention. They are organized into the following chapters: How Serious Is the Problem of Gun Violence? Does Private Ownership of Handguns Increase the Threat of Gun Violence? Does the Constitution Protect Private Gun Ownership? How Can Gun Violence Be Reduced? The school shootings in Pearl, Littleton, and other towns such as Paducah, Kentucky, and Jonesboro, Arkansas, were tragic. But they have served to raise the level of debate over the problem of gun violence, as other high-profile shootings have in the past.

CHAPTER 1

How Serious Is the Problem of Gun Violence?

Chapter Preface

The good news regarding gun violence is that it is in decline. In November 1999 the FBI reported that gun deaths in the United States dropped 21 percent between 1993 and 1997 to the lowest level in more than thirty years, and firearm-related injuries fell 41 percent. Survey figures from the FBI indicate that major violent and property crimes reported to police dropped again in 1999, down 7 percent from the year before. Experts cite a variety of factors that may have contributed to lower levels of gun violence, including tougher gun control laws, a booming economy, better police work, increasing rates of incarceration, declining crack and cocaine use, and a dip in the number of young males, the group most prone to violent crime.

But despite this decline, the public's perception that gun violence is a serious problem seems to be growing: *American Demographics* magazine reported in April 2000 that 70 percent of Americans believe crime rates are rising. While that perception is not exactly accurate, it is understandable. Despite some recent declines, the United States still leads the industrialized world in levels of gun violence. And the FBI estimates that 83 percent of Americans can expect to be victims of violent or property crime at least once in their lifetimes. High-profile shootings such as the one in Littleton, Colorado, have also contributed to growing fears of gun violence.

"People shouldn't be satisfied," said Nancy Hwa, a spokeswoman for Handgun Control Inc., "Everybody is still at risk, and the presence of guns should still be a major concern." On the other hand, *Boston Globe* columnist Cathy Young believes it is important to keep the problem of gun violence in perspective: "Gun fatalities have been declining for years. More can probably be done to reduce gun violence. But to make real progress, we must approach the issue with a clear understanding of facts, . . . without turning the gun debate into a morality play pitting the forces of good against the forces of evil." The authors in the following chapter further debate the extent of gun violence in America.

"The call to ban handguns . . . is a response to the blood price that our nation has paid for the explosive growth of the handgun population."

Gun Violence
Is a Serious Problem

Violence Policy Center

In the following viewpoint, the Violence Policy Center (VPC) provides an array of statistics on gun violence—particularly handgun violence—in the United States. The VPC argues that America's high levels of handgun-related homicide, suicide, accidental shooting, and injury justify a ban on civilian ownership of handguns. The VPC asserts that handguns are rarely used in self-defense and that therefore their purported benefits are minor compared to the enormous harm they cause. The VPC is a national educational organization that works to reduce gun death and injury in America by promoting awareness about the problem of gun violence.

As you read, consider the following questions:

1. What was the firearms death rate in the United States in 1995, as compared to Canada, Australia, and England, as cited in the viewpoint?
2. According to the VPC, what percent of handgun homicides in 1997 were classified as justifiable homicides?
3. What type of death accounts for the majority of gun deaths, according to the VPC?

Reprinted, with permission, from "Unsafe in Any Hands: Why America Needs to Ban Handguns," a study by the Violence Policy Center, 2000, available at http://www.vpc.org/studies/unsafe.htm.

The United States leads the industrialized world in firearms violence of all types—homicides, suicides, and unintentional deaths. Most of this violence involves the use of a handgun. Handguns are easily concealed, engineered for maximum lethality, relatively inexpensive, and easy to acquire. On average, handguns are used in nearly 70 percent of firearm suicides and 80 percent of firearm homicides. The United States has not so much a firearms problem as a handgun problem.

The Toll of Handgun Violence

The call to ban handguns is not inspired by a generalized hatred of guns. It is a response to the blood price that our nation has paid for the explosive growth of the handgun population over the past generation. More than two out of three of the one million Americans who died in firearm-related homicides, suicides, and unintentional shootings since 1962 were killed with handguns—i.e., 667,000. This weapon, which has inflicted pain and death in such a disproportionate degree, is owned by a distinct minority of Americans—only one out of six adults. Out of the current total firearms population of some 190 million, rifles and shotguns outnumber handguns two to one, yet handguns account for the majority of killings, woundings, and gun crimes. For example, of all firearm-related crimes in 1993, 86 percent involved the use of a handgun.

The modern handgun has been honed for decades by the firearms industry to the highest possible level of lethality, just as race cars are continually redeveloped for maximum speed. The handguns that have been introduced into the market in the past two decades—especially high-caliber, high-capacity, semiautomatic pistols—meet the lethality standard admirably. The increased efficiency of the handgun as a killing machine is the result of a strategy by the gun industry over the past decade and a half to boost sales. This growth in killing power is the result of three variables deliberately designed into handguns—

- Greater *capacity*, i.e. the ability to hold more bullets.
- Higher *caliber*, meaning bigger bullets.
- Increased *concealability*, facilitating criminal use.

These variables reached their zenith with the recent introduction of "pocket rockets,"—semiautomatic pistols in higher calibers that can be concealed in the palm of the hand.

Handgun Homicides and Injuries

Recent data reveal the effect of this decades-long trend. From 1990 to 1997, of the 160,000 homicides committed in the United States, more than half (55.6 percent) involved a handgun. This block of 89,000 handgun homicides is larger than that of all other weapons used in homicides *combined.*

As the debate over gun violence is almost always framed in terms of fatalities, it is easy to overlook that, for every person killed with a firearm, approximately three others require medical treatment for wounds inflicted with a gun. One conservative estimate places the annual cost of immediate medical care for all gunshot wounds at $4 billion. Other researchers take into account lifetime care and long-term economic loss, calculating the overall cost of gun violence in any given year to be in excess of $20 billion. Statistics for the costs of handgun violence in particular are not available. Nonetheless, since handguns cause the majority of firearm injuries, it follows that handgun injuries are responsible for the majority of firearm-related expenses.

There are an estimated 65 million handguns in America. The deleterious impact of this large handgun population on our murder rate becomes evident when making comparisons to countries that strongly regulate private firearms ownership with an emphasis on minimizing access to handguns. For example, in 1995 the U.S. firearms death rate was 13.7 per 100,000; in Canada 3.9 per 100,000; in Australia 2.9 per 100,000; and, in England and Wales it was 0.4 per 100,000. Contrary to a common rationalization, the United States is not especially more violent than other "older" cultures; in fact, as Western Europe grows more violent, the U.S. becomes less so. The main difference between those nations and our own is that we have more than 60 million handguns. The lesson to be learned from this is, as one public health researcher stated: "People without guns *injure* people; guns *kill* them."

The mythology woven around the handgun by the gun

lobby clouds the reality that a handgun is a consumer product that ought to be judged and regulated by the same standards applied to all other products. However, the firearms industry is exempt from basic federal consumer product health and safety regulation. Aside from the issuance of pro forma licenses for gun manufacturers and dealers, no federal agency has the authority to review the firearm industry's products in terms of their relative costs and benefits. Using this cost/benefit standard, two reasonable and essential questions need to be posed about the handgun—

- Is it innately dangerous to the user or to anyone else?
- What does its use cost society in human and monetary terms in contrast to its beneficial applications?

Indeed, by making a simple comparison between the costs of civilian handgun ownership versus the benefits these weapons are purported to deliver, the case for banning handguns becomes self-evident. For example, for every time in 1997 that a civilian used a handgun to kill in self-defense, 43 people lost their lives in handgun homicides alone. This passes any point of rational justification for condoning the existence of such a product on the open market, especially in an unregulated state.

An Ineffective Means of Self-Defense

Through the use of dubious methodologies, the National Rifle Association and other pro-gun advocates have created wildly inflated numbers supposedly showing handguns to be an effective means of self-defense. This claim is false. Although handguns are marketed primarily for their self-defense value, bringing one into the home has exactly the opposite effect, placing residents at a much higher rate of risk. A person living in a home with a gun is three times more likely to die by homicide and five times more likely to die by suicide.

Data from 1997 buttress the point that self-defense handgun uses are rare. In that year there was—

- A total of 15,690 homicides.
- Of these, 8,503 (54.2 percent) were committed with handguns, contrasted to 2,207 involving *all other types of firearms* (14.1 percent).
- Among handgun homicides, only 193 (2.3 percent) were

classified as justifiable homicides by civilians.

For decades handguns have been marketed and purchased as the strongest bulwark a law-abiding citizen could have against a legion of dangerous strangers. However, of the 8,503 handgun homicides in 1997, only 110 (1.3 percent) were justifiable killings of an assailant previously unknown to the person using a handgun. Instances in which a person uses a handgun in self-defense against an unknown attacker do occur, but compared against the total universe of gun crime and violence, they are extremely rare.

Handguns are employed extensively in violent crimes such as assaults and robberies. In 1993 there were about 1.3 million such crimes committed with a firearm—and 86 percent of the time the weapon was a handgun. Conversely, an analysis of four years of National Crime Victimization Survey (NCVS) data indicated that gun owners claim to defend themselves with a firearm of any type approximately 65,000 times in an average year—a minute percentage compared to the total figure for violent crime.

Contrary to the National Rifle Association's standard portrayal of gun violence, most gun deaths do not take place during the course of felony crime. Considering what the FBI has been reporting year in and year out—that most homicides result from arguments between people who know each other—it is clear that a handgun purchased for self-protection poses the gravest danger to the very person it is supposed to protect.

Suicide and Unintended Shootings

Throughout the long and bitter debate over gun violence, the fact that the largest number of gun deaths is suicides, not homicides, has been consistently overlooked. For example, from 1990 to 1997 there were 147,000 suicides committed with a firearm in contrast to 100,000 firearm homicides. An estimated 90,000 of these suicides were accomplished with a handgun—a tribute to the operational simplicity and high lethality that make it the ideal suicide machine. Perhaps because of a lingering sense of suicide as a shameful act, this calamitous by-product of handgun ownership has been largely disregarded by even gun control advocates. Obviously handguns by themselves do not make people suicidal. But their ready availability has increased their use in suicide attempts and the use of a firearm all but guarantees that a suicide attempt will end in a fatality.

International Homicide Rates for Children

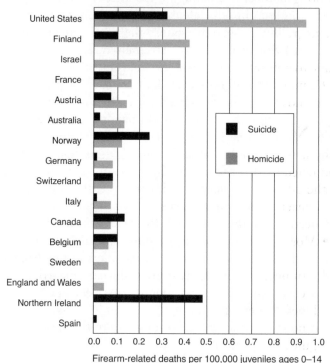

Firearm-related deaths per 100,000 juveniles ages 0–14

Office of Juvenile Justice and Delinquency Prevention, "Kids and Guns," *Juvenile Justice Bulletin*, March 2000.

People living in a household with a gun are five times more likely to commit suicide than those living in a gun-free home—and seven times out of 10 a handgun will be their weapon of choice. The deadly link between handgun ownership and suicide was decisively established in a 1999 study of California handgun purchasers showing that the suicide rate during the first week after the purchase of a handgun is 57 *times higher* than for the population as a whole. During the first year after purchase, suicide remained the leading cause of death among handgun purchasers.

In sharp contrast, unintentional shootings involving children, which receive the lion's share of media attention, actually generate the smallest number of firearm deaths in any category. In 1997 there were 981 victims of unintentional shooting deaths, of whom 142 were aged 14 years old or younger. Regardless of the means, the violent death of a young person is a catastrophe, but it is still important to note that, while 300 young people between the ages of 15 years to 24 years old died in unintentional shootings in 1997, more than eight times as many died in firearms suicides, most involving handguns. . . .

The Need for a National Ban on Handguns

Why has more than 30 years of federal gun control legislation failed to slow the carnage? This is in large measure due to the ad hoc nature in which gun control legislation has been enacted often in response to specific acts of violence.

Effective legislation must take into account the following—
- Most victims know their killers and are often related to them.
- Criminals often get their guns through gun stores and are skilled in evading point-of-purchase legal roadblocks.
- The secondary gun market—i.e., the selling of guns at gun shows or over the Internet—is in reality totally unregulated.
- It is the self-defense handgun purchased by "law-abiding" citizens that ends up being used in most handgun violence.

Politicians and gun control advocates alike, however, have a tendency to proffer the same legislative remedies over and over ("licensing and registration" or "background checks") without consideration of these fundamentals or inquiry into the actual effects such laws might have on reducing firearms violence overall. . . .

If a handgun ban were enacted, what should be done about the existing supply of some 65 million civilian-owned handguns? Could the nation afford to eliminate them through a program? Since many handguns began as cheap "junk guns," a generous estimate of the average buy-back price would be $250. The total tab would be about $16.25 billion, which is slightly more than three SSN-21 nuclear attack submarines. Considering that by conservative estimates America spends $4 billion annually on medical care for gun violence victims, the cost of a buy-back could be recouped in a few years.

A clear-cut plan to ban handguns should be developed and implemented soon. Considering the many thousands who are killed or maimed by the handgun each year, how much more motivation do we need?

"A full listing of the lies told by the antigun lobby could fill a book."

Gun Control Advocates Exaggerate the Extent of Gun Violence

Dave Kopel

In the following viewpoint, Dave Kopel asserts that antigun organizations and activists often misrepresent the facts concerning gun violence. He cites several statistics often used in gun control arguments and argues that they are exaggerated and misleading. He further argues that some claims made by antigun forces—such as the charge that firearms sales at gun shows are not regulated—are outright lies. Kopel maintains that gun violence should be put in perspective. For example, he notes, most gun violence is committed by criminals. Kopel is research director of the Independence Institute, a free-market think tank in Colorado that opposes gun control legislation.

As you read, consider the following questions:
1. About how many children do gun control advocates claim are killed each day by guns, according to Kopel, and what is the actual daily death rate?
2. Why is it misleading to claim that most gun homicides take place among acquaintances, in the author's opinion?
3. What is wrong with the claim that owning a gun is associated with a higher risk of being murdered, in Kopel's view?

Reprinted, with permission, from Dave Kopel, "An Army of Gun Lies," *National Review*, April 17, 2000. Copyright © 2000 by National Review, Inc., 215 Lexington Ave., New York, NY 10016.

Antigun advocates have always faced an uphill battle in this country. Americans have, to begin with, a constitutional right to gun ownership. Today, half of American households exercise this right, owning a total of about 250 million guns; and over 99 percent of those households do so in a responsible manner. To fight for major restrictions on an item that plays such a valued part in the lives of so many people looks like a nearly impossible task. So if you're really committed to the effort, and you want to win, what do you do?

Simple: You lie.

Counting Teenagers as Children

A full listing of the lies told by the antigun lobby could fill a book. A short list of the more popular ones would have to begin with the canard about the number of children killed by firearms. We are told repeatedly that 13, or 15, or 17 children every day are killed by guns. This factoid is used to conjure up pictures of dozens of little kids dying in gun accidents every week.

In truth, the number of fatal gun accidents is at its lowest level since 1903, when statistics started being kept. That's right: Not only is the per capita accident rate at a record low, so is the actual number of accidents—even though the number of people and the number of guns are both much larger than in 1903.

The assertions about "X children per day" are based on counting older teenagers, or even people in their early twenties, as "children." The claims are true only if you count a 19-year-old drug dealer who is shot by a competitor, or an 18-year-old armed robber who is shot by a policeman, as "a child killed by a gun." As for actual children (14 years and under), the daily death rate is 2.6. For children ten and under, it's 0.4 per day—far lower than the number of children who are killed by automobiles, drowning, or many other causes.

The Myth of the Gun-Show Loophole

If the statistic about child gun deaths is the most notorious lie, one of the most frequent has to do with gun shows. All of the antigun groups repeat, incessantly, the phrase "gun-show loophole." As a result, much of the public believes that gun shows are special zones exempt from ordinary gun laws. Handgun Control, Inc., the major antigun group, has an affiliate in Colorado that claims that the "vast majority" of guns used in crimes come from gun shows, while the Violence Policy Center calls gun shows "Tupperware parties for criminals."

This is all an audacious lie. First of all, the laws at gun shows are exactly the same as they are everywhere else. If a person is "engaged in the business" (as the law puts it) of selling firearms, then he must fill out a government registration form on every buyer, and get FBI permission (through the National Instant Check System) for every sale—regardless of whether the sale takes place at his gun store, at an office in his home, or at a gun show. Those who are not gun dealers by profession, but happen to be selling a gun, are not required to follow this procedure. To imply that gun dealers can go to an event called a "gun show" and thus avoid the law is absolutely false.

Also false is the charge about Tupperware parties for criminals. According to a National Institute of Justice study released in December 1997, only 2 percent of guns used in crimes come from gun shows.

The Reality of Firearm Homicide

The gun-show charge has great currency in the media, but it is not very important in itself. How about the more serious charge that guns are basically dangerous to society? Public-health experts and gun-control lobbyists will tell you that most murders, including those involving guns, take place among acquaintances and are perpetrated by ordinary people; these facts supposedly indicate that ordinary people are too hot-tempered to be allowed to have guns.

The facts tell a different story: 75 percent of murderers have adult criminal records. As for the rest, a large number either have criminal convictions as juveniles or are still teenagers when they commit the murder; laws dealing with access to juvenile-crime records prevent full access to their rap sheets. Furthermore, the category of "acquaintance" murders is misleading. It includes drug buyers who kill a drug dealer to steal his stash, and thugs who assault each other in barroom brawls.

There's also a sad irony here. Domestic murders are almost always preceded by many incidents of violent abuse. If a domestic-violence victim flees the home, and her exhusband tracks her down and tries to rape her, and she shoots him, the killing will be labeled a "tragic domestic homicide that was caused by a gun," rather than what it legally is: justifiable use of deadly force against a felon.

Bogus Statistics on Gun Ownership

The famous factoid that a gun in the home is 43 times more likely to kill a family member than to kill a criminal is predicated on a similar misclassification. Of the 43 deaths, 37 are suicides; and while there are obviously many ways in which a person can commit suicide, only a gun allows a small woman a realistic opportunity to defend herself at a distance from a large male predator.

Emory University medical professor Arthur Kellermann is a one-man factory of this type of misleading data. One of his most famous studies purported to show that owning a gun is associated with a 2.7 times greater risk of being murdered. Kellermann compared murder victims in several

---

Antigun Bias in Media Coverage of Gun Violence

In a study of 653 morning and evening news stories on ABC, CBS, CNN, and NBC from July 1, 1997 to June 30, 1999, Media Research Center (MRC) Senior Media Analyst Geoffrey Dickens documents how:

1. TV News Has Chosen Sides. Stories advocating more gun control outnumbered stories opposing gun control by 357 to 36, or a ratio of almost 10 to 1. (Another 260 were neutral.) . . .

2. News Programs Are Twice as Likely to Use Anti-Gun Soundbites. Anti-gun soundbites were twice as frequent as pro-gun ones—412 to 209. (Another 471 were neutral.)

3. News Programs Are Twice as Likely to Feature Anti-Gun Guests. In morning show interview segments, gun control advocates appeared as guests on 82 occasions, compared to just 37 for gun-rights activists and 58 neutral spokesmen.

Media Research Center, "Outgunned: How the Network News Media Are Spinning the Gun Control Debate—Executive Summary," January 5, 2000, www.mediaresearch.org/specialreports/news/sr2000105.html.

---

cities with sociologically similar people a few blocks away in those cities, who had not been murdered.

The 2.7 factoid was trumpeted all over the country; but the study is patently illogical. First of all, Kellermann's own data show that owning a security system, or renting a home rather than owning it, are also associated with equally large increased risks of death. Yet newspapers did not start running dire stories warning people to rip out their burglar alarms or to start lobbying their condo association to dissolve. The 2.7 factoid also overlooks the obvious fact that one reason people choose to own guns, or to install burglar alarms, is that they are already at higher risk of being victimized by crime. As Yale law professor John Lott points out, Kellermann's methodology is like comparing 100 people who went to a hospital in a given year with 100 similar people who did not, finding that more of the hospital patients died, and then announcing that hospitals increase the risk of death. Kellermann's method would also prove that possession of insulin increases the risk of diabetes.

"Assault Weapon" Hysteria

The media are complicit in many of these lies. Take, for example, the hysteria about so-called "assault weapons." Almost everything that gun-control advocates say about these firearms is a lie. The guns in question are not machine guns; they are simply ordinary guns with ugly cosmetics that give them a pseudo-military appearance. The guns do not fire faster than ordinary guns. The bullets they fire are not especially powerful; they are, in fact, smaller and travel at lower velocity than bullets from standard hunting rifles.

The media have succeeded in giving a totally different impression—through deliberate fraud. The CBS show *48 Hours* purported to show a semiautomatic rifle being converted to fully automatic—i.e., turned into a machine gun—in just nine minutes. But the gun shown at the beginning was not the same gun that was fired at the end of the demonstration. An expert from the Bureau of Alcohol, Tobacco and Firearms (BATF) later said that such a conversion was impossible. And in Denver, KMGH television filmed people firing automatic weapons and told viewers that the guns were semiautomatics.

The chief culprits are not the media but the antigun lob-byists themselves, some of whom have very little compunc-tion about lying—even in cases where it can be proven rather easily that they are aware of the truth while spread-ing the falsehood. For example, in February 1989, a former BATF employee who had become a paid consultant for Handgun Control testified to Congress that "assault weapons" were rarely used in crimes. (He wanted to ban them anyway, as a precautionary measure.) Nevertheless, within weeks, Handgun Control was running an advertising campaign insisting that assault weapons were the criminal weapons of choice.

The Dishonesty of Antigun Groups

The most dangerous dishonesty concerns the ultimate in-tentions of the antigun forces. Handgun Control claims that it merely wants to "keep guns out of the wrong hands"; yet in 1999, it lobbied hard to preserve Washington, D.C.'s out-right ban on handguns. Back in 1976, the group's then leader, Pete Shields, explained the long-term strategy to *The New Yorker*: "The first problem is to slow down the number of handguns being produced and sold in this country. The second problem is to get handguns registered. The final problem is to make possession of all handguns and all hand-gun ammunition—except for the military, police, licensed security guards, licensed sporting clubs, and licensed gun collectors—totally illegal."

Sarah Brady, the current chairwoman of Handgun Con-trol, has said that people should not be allowed to own guns for self-defense. Yet in debates, employees of the group steadfastly deny that the organization believes in the policies articulated by its leaders.

In short, they are lying about what they want to accom-plish. This is understandable, to be sure; but not honorable, or right for the country.

"The rate of firearm deaths among children under age 15 is almost 12 times higher in the United States than in 25 other industrialized countries combined."

Gun Violence Among Youth Is a Serious Problem

Children's Defense Fund

The following viewpoint is excerpted from *Protect Children Instead of Guns 2000*, a report from the Children's Defense Fund (CDF). In it, the CDF details the statistics regarding children and firearm violence. The CDF acknowledges that firearm-related fatalities among children have been declining since the mid-1990s, but maintains that rates of gun violence among children are still staggeringly high. The CDF details the problems of gun homicide, suicide, and accidental injury among children and teenagers, and concludes that new federal gun laws are necessary to protect children from gun violence. The Children's Defense Fund is a nonprofit organization that works to insure the health and well-being of children.

As you read, consider the following questions:
1. According to the CDF, what percentage of children killed by gunfire are victims of homicide?
2. In what proportion of youth suicides are guns used, as cited by the viewpoint?
3. What was the Million Mom March, as described by the CDF?

The latest data released in 2000 show that in a single year 3,761 children and teens were killed by gunfire in the United States—that's one child almost every two and a half hours, 10 children every day, more than 70 children every week. Between 1979 and 1998, gunfire killed nearly 84,000 children and teens in America—36,000 more than the total number of American soldiers killed in battle in Vietnam. In the United States, firearms outnumber children by a margin of almost three to one. It's time to stop protecting the approximately 200 million firearms in our country and start protecting the nearly 75 million American children and teens under age 19. It's time for a *real* gun safety policy in America. It's time to protect children instead of guns.

Between 1994 and 1998, youth firearm deaths dropped 35 percent after peaking in 1994 at 5,793 young lives. Since 1994, the number of Black children and teens killed by guns has decreased 45 percent, and the number of Whites has dropped 28 percent. Although it is encouraging that the number of child gun deaths per year has dropped below 4,000 for the first time since 1988, the number remains disturbingly high. We are still losing too many children. When compared to other industrialized countries, the numbers are even more staggering. According to the Centers for Disease Control and Prevention, the rate of firearm deaths among children under age 15 is almost 12 times higher in the United States than in 25 other industrialized countries combined. American children are 16 times more likely to be murdered with a gun, 11 times more likely to commit suicide with a gun, and nine times more likely to die in a firearm accident than children in these other countries. The impact of gun violence on children is, in many ways, a uniquely American phenomenon—a shameful distinction for the world's wealthiest and most powerful nation.

Homicide—Behind the Decline

Fifty-eight percent of young people killed by gunfire are victims of homicide. In 1998, homicide accounted for 2,184 deaths among children age 19 and younger. Although the decrease in firearm homicides accounted for most of the decrease in child firearm deaths from 1997 to 1998, not all communities are experiencing the decline. Many large cities, such as New York, Miami, and Boston, have experienced a decline in homicide rates over the last several years, but Baltimore's murder rate has remained stagnant. Underlying this disturbing trend is evidence that gun violence victims in Baltimore are getting younger. In 1999, Johns Hopkins Hospital treated 390 gunshot wounds, more than one a day, and almost two-thirds of the patients were between 15 and 20 years old.

Suicide—The Overlooked Crisis

Although most child gun deaths are homicides, two out of every five young firearm deaths are the result of suicide or an accidental shooting. Thirty-three percent of young people killed by guns take their own lives. In 1998, suicide accounted for 1,241 child and teen firearm deaths—an average of more than three every day. Between 1997 and 1998, the percent of child firearm deaths attributable to homicide declined, but the percentage of firearm suicide deaths increased. Guns are used in two out of three youth suicides and, unlike other attempted methods, are the most likely to be fatal. This is particularly notable considering federal law requires individuals be at least 21 years old to purchase a handgun, and more than 20 states have some minimum age requirement for the possession of rifles and long guns. So, where are children getting these guns? Unfortunately, in most cases, the weapons come from their own homes or from someone they know. More than two-thirds of firearms involved in self-inflicted firearm injuries and deaths come from either the victim's home or the home of a friend or relative.

Accidental Deaths—The Easiest Tragedy to Prevent

Accidental shootings accounted for about seven percent of child firearm deaths in 1998; 262 children and teens lost their lives in accidental shootings. America loses the equivalent of 25 youth basketball teams each year because a gun was left unlocked, loaded, and too easy for the wrong hands to reach. As with adolescent suicide, a vast majority of firearms used in unintentional shootings of children and teens come from the victim's home or the home of a relative, friend, or parent of a friend of the victim. A study reported in the *American Journal of Public Health* found that 1.4 million homes with 2.6 million children had firearms that were stored unlocked and loaded or unlocked and unloaded but stored with ammunition. A recent survey found that most gun-owning parents store their firearms loaded or unlocked, believing that their child can properly handle a gun and can tell the difference between a toy gun and a real gun.

America Needs a *Real* Policy on Gun Safety

On Mother's Day 2000, hundreds of thousands of mothers, grandmothers, daughters, sisters, and others gathered on the National Mall in Washington, DC as part of the Million Mom March to urge the country to change fundamentally how guns are regarded and regulated. Hundreds of women shared personal stories of tragedies related to gun violence at the largest public rally against gun violence in the nation's history. These women and their families called on our national leaders to do more to protect our children—not just through greater enforcement of gun crime, but through a comprehensive, national policy to ensure every child's right to a safe, gun-free environment. It's time for a *real* gun safety policy that reaches children in all states. To protect children instead of guns, we must insist on national legislation to:

Register All Firearms and License All Gun Owners

What does this mean?

• Require gun owners to register their firearms. Much like motor vehicle registration, a registration system for firearms will help police track the transfer of firearms that end up in the hands of children or those who would harm children. Requiring registration at *all* points of sale would ensure that background checks are conducted to make certain that gun buyers are not legally prohibited from owning a firearm. Such a system will help create a heightened responsibility and greater accountability for firearm ownership.

• Require potential gun owners to obtain a license in order to purchase or use a firearm. Much like a driver's license for operating an automobile, a licensing system for gun owners would require applicants to pass competence and safety

Firearm Homicide by Juveniles

Based on the Federal Bureau of Investigation's (FBI's) Supplemental Homicide Report (SHR) data, 18,200 persons were murdered in the U.S. in 1997—the lowest number in more than a generation. Of these murders, about 1,400 were determined by law enforcement to involve a juvenile offender. . . .

Whom do juveniles kill?

Between 1980 and 1997, most victims in homicides involving juveniles were male (83%). Slightly more victims were white (50%) than black (47%). In 27% of homicides by juveniles, the victim was also a juvenile. Victims in 70% of homicides by juveniles were killed with a firearm. Of all victims killed by juveniles, 14% were family members, 55% were acquaintances, and 31% were strangers.

Who are the juvenile murderers?

Between 1980 and 1997, the large majority (93%) of known juvenile homicide offenders were male. More than half (56%) were black. Of known juvenile homicide offenders, 42% were age 17, 29% were age 16, and 17% were age 15; 88% of juvenile homicide offenders were age 15 or older.

Office of Juvenile Justice and Delinquency Prevention, "Kids and Guns," *Juvenile Justice Bulletin*, March 2000.

---

tests before being allowed to use or own a gun.

How will it help?

• Registration will increase accountability for firearm owners who transfer or sell their firearm illegally or irresponsibly. Not only will registration help law enforcement's ability to trace weapons used in crime and hold individuals accountable for the illegal use of firearms, it will create a higher standard of responsibility for gun ownership to keep firearms out of the hands of children and those who would harm them.

• Similarly, licensing will ensure that gun owners know how to safely use and store their firearm and understand the consequences of allowing access to weapons by children and individuals not permitted to own or use firearms.

• Both licensing and registration will make it more difficult for the angry or depressed individual to impulsively buy a handgun to harm themselves or someone else. Massachusetts is the only state that has both licensing and registration for all firearms.

Encourage Safe Storage Laws and Mandatory Trigger Locks

What does this mean?

• Require safety devices, such as trigger locks, be sold with all new guns to prevent children from being able to load and fire them.

• Encourage state legislatures to enact Child Access Prevention (CAP) laws that call for strict penalties for adults who allow children access to firearms regardless of whether injury results.

How will it help?

• Safe storage devices, such as trigger locks, can prevent children and teens from accessing and operating firearms. Just five states—California, Connecticut, Massachusetts, New Jersey, and Hawaii—have passed legislation requiring that safe storage devices be sold with all new gun purchases.

• Safe storage policies help to ensure responsible gun ownership by adults. The estimated number of households with guns is as high as 40 percent, and one out of every three handguns is kept loaded and unlocked. A study published in the *Journal of the American Medical Association* found that twelve states that have enacted CAP laws have witnessed a 23 percent drop in accidental shootings of children between 1990 and 1994. Based on this 1997 study, an estimated 216 children killed in unintentional shootings would still be alive today if CAP laws were in effect in every state. Eighteen states have enacted CAP laws since 1989.

Apply Consumer Safety Standards to the Gun Industry

What does this mean?

• The gun industry is currently exempt from any consumer safety features. Toy guns and teddy bears are more regulated and must meet more rigorous safety standards than firearms.

How will it help?

• Oversight based on uniform standards will ensure that design flaws are identified and corrected and that simple and often inexpensive safety features, such as devices that show whether the chamber is loaded and internal trigger locks, are incorporated in the manufacture of the firearm. Massachusetts is the first and only state in the nation that has taken steps to impose consumer safety regulations on firearms.

Limit Handgun Purchases to One a Month

What does this mean?

• In order to combat the practice of "gun-running," where an individual can purchase an unrestricted quantity of firearms and transport them to a state with weaker gun laws, several states have enacted one-gun-a-month policies that limit gun buyers to one gun purchase in a 30-day period.

How will it help?

• By prohibiting one-time purchases of multiple firearms, the practice of transporting massive numbers of firearms to illegal markets, known as gun-running, will be significantly curbed. Currently, only four states—California, Maryland, South Carolina, and Virginia—have a one-gun-a-month law limiting firearm purchases.

| "Researchers found substantial declines in violence at high schools in the 1990s."

The Problem of Gun Violence Among Youth Is Exaggerated

Barry Glassner

The following viewpoint was written in August 1999, in response to several public shootings that occurred in U.S. cities that month, as well as the shootings at Columbine High School in April 1999. In it, Barry Glassner argues that while these shootings are tragic, parents' concerns about increased gun violence among youth are unfounded. He cites federal statistics indicating that violent crime among youth is down and that fewer students report bringing firearms to school than in the past. Nevertheless, he asserts, the media hype surrounding Columbine and other school shootings has led students to feel less safe at school. Glassner maintains that the exaggerated scare about youth violence has drawn attention away from other important dangers to youth. Glassner is the author of *The Culture of Fear: Why Americans Are Afraid of the Wrong Things*.

As you read, consider the following questions:
1. According to the Centers for Disease Control, as cited by Glassner, the number of students who said they carry a gun to school fell by what percent from 1991 to 1997?
2. How has Congressman Bill McCollum referred to violent juvenile crime, as quoted by the author?
3. What does the author say are the biggest risks to young people?

The sight of children fleeing a gunman at a Jewish center in Los Angeles on Tuesday [August 10, 1999,] terrified parents everywhere. Coming as it did after two workplace killing sprees in the South in the last few weeks, the latest violence only heightened concern about security as schools prepare to open this month. Several newscasts paired footage of the children being led away from the community center with clips of students fleeing Columbine High School last April.

School Violence Is Down

But parents, lawmakers and pundits would do well to keep in mind the auspicious findings from a study conducted by researchers from the Centers for Disease Control, published in the *Journal of the American Medical Association*. The researchers found substantial declines in violence at high schools in the 1990's. From 1991 to 1997, the number of high school students who said they carried a gun fell 25 percent. Over the same period, the number of students who said they had been involved in a fight at school decreased by 9 percent.

These trends are backed up by other research. The Department of Education reported recently that 30 percent fewer students were expelled for bringing firearms to school during the 1997-98 academic year than in the previous year. And the Justice Department reported that the number of violent crimes committed by children and teenagers has declined substantially since 1993 and is at the lowest rate since 1986.

The Hysteria Inspired by School Shootings

But these facts will probably not stop parents and children from believing that America is experiencing a plague of youth violence. As a result, even as students report fewer weapons and fights, they do not feel safer. On the contrary, surveys conducted by the Horatio Alger Association of Distinguished Americans, a nonprofit group, found that the number of public school students who said they always feel safe in school fell from 44 percent in 1998 to 37 percent this year.

Other studies show that adults are fearful of teen-agers as well. In a national survey on social issues conducted by the

Wall Street Journal and NBC News in June [1999], 58 percent of respondents ranked youth violence as a top concern. Only 38 percent selected the nearest contender, Internet pornography and privacy issues.

It's no wonder that Americans remain fearful and confused about youth violence: the hot rhetoric of politicians and ceaseless news coverage are enough to convince anyone that the problem is getting worse.

For instance, Bill McCollum, a Republican Representative from Florida, has referred to violent juvenile crime as "a national epidemic" and violent youths as "feral, presocial beings." Democrats have been just as guilty of using overblown language. They claimed, for example, that their Republican colleagues would have blood on their hands if they failed to pass gun control legislation before the new school year, even though the proposed measures stood little chance of preventing campus shootings.

Firearm Homicides by Juveniles Are Declining

Homicides known to involve juvenile offenders

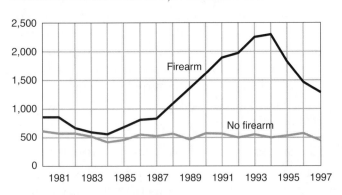

Office of Juvenile Justice and Delinquency Prevention, "Kids and Guns," *Juvenile Justice Bulletin*, March 2000.

Anyone watching the news would find it almost impossible to believe that school violence has decreased. The opening of Columbine High School next week has provided another opportunity to reprise the frightening pictures from shootings of the past couple of years. As more schools open, we can expect to hear about every young person who threatens to shoot at or bomb his school.

Sadly, we can also expect that there will be additional shootings. In a nation of nearly 53 million students, it would be surprising if none opted for fame through martyrdom or were homicidal psychotics.

Exaggerating the Problem Is Counterproductive

Without question, this small minority of young people can cause great damage. But exaggerated scares about youthful violence can be dangerous, too.

Not only does the hoopla inspire copycat crimes and motivate people to arm themselves in self-defense, but it also directs attention and money away from the biggest risks to young people—accidents, particularly car crashes, and poverty. With 20 percent of American children living in poverty and thousands dying each year in accidents that could be prevented, our preoccupation with teen killers does our country a profound disservice.

Periodical Bibliography

The following articles have been selected to supplement the diverse views presented in this chapter. Addresses are provided for periodicals not indexed in the *Readers' Guide to Periodical Literature*, the *Alternative Press Index*, the *Social Sciences Index*, or the *Index to Legal Periodicals and Books*.

Brian Bremner	"Guns Are Wounding America's Image Abroad," *Business Week*, August 16, 1999.
Business Week	"Say Yes to Serious Gun Control," August 16, 1999.
Fox Butterfield	"F.B.I. Study Finds Gun Use in Violent Crimes Declining," *New York Times*, October 18, 1999.
Dana Charry and Ellen Charry	"The Crisis of Violence," *Christian Century*, July 15, 1998.
Christianity Today	"In Guns We Trust," October 4, 1999.
Congressional Digest	"Firearms in America: The Link Between Guns and Violence," November 1999.
Glamour	"Kids Gunning Down Kids," July 1999.
Laura Helmuth	"Has America's Tide of Violence Receded for Good?" *Science*, July 28, 2000.
Issues and Controversies on File	"Gun Control," July 14, 2000.
Roger Rosenblatt	"Get Rid of the Damned Things," *Time*, August 9, 1999.
Kenneth Smith	"Loaded Coverage: How the News Media Miss the Mark on the Gun Issue," *Reason*, June 2000.
Andrew Stuttaford	"Moms Away: The New Brand of Gun Nut," *National Review*, June 5, 2000.

CHAPTER 2

Does Private Ownership of Handguns Increase the Threat of Gun Violence?

Chapter Preface

One spark that has reignited the debate over gun violence in recent years was the 1998 publication of Yale economist John R. Lott Jr.'s provocatively titled book *More Guns, Less Crime*. In it, Lott challenges the conventional wisdom regarding gun violence by arguing that communities are safer when more people are allowed to own and carry guns. He and researcher David Mustard compared crime data from ten states and found that violent crime rates were lower in states that allow virtually all gun owners to obtain permits to carry concealed weapons in public. "Criminals are motivated by self-preservation, and handguns can therefore be a deterrent," explains Lott. "When guns are concealed, criminals are unable to tell whether the victim is armed before striking, which raises the risk to criminals of committing many types of crimes." Gun rights organizations—who have long pointed to individual stories of guns being used to stop, rather than commit, crimes—hailed Lott's book as definitive proof that gun ownership is a positive force in society.

But Lott's research also received a storm of criticism, both from gun control groups and academics. Daniel Webster of the Berkeley Media Studies Group notes that Lott's study "does not adequately control for many other factors that are almost surely relevant for a state's crime rate, including poverty, drugs . . . , gang activity, and police resources or strategies." Gary Kleck, a prominent researcher on guns and crime, also disputes the findings. He writes in his book *Targeting Guns*, "The declines in crime, coinciding with relaxation of carry laws were largely attributable to other factors not controlled for in the Lott and Mustard analysis." "Until proven otherwise, the best science indicates that more guns will lead to more deaths," concludes Webster.

The controversy over carrying concealed handguns is just one of the issues to consider when weighing the benefits of gun ownership against the risks. The authors in the following chapter debate whether owning a gun increases or decreases an individual's risk of becoming a victim of gun violence.

> "The simple fact is that murder and other crimes committed with firearms occur more frequently where guns are most plentiful."

Gun Ownership Contributes to Violent Crime

C. Emory Burton

C. Emory Burton, a retired United Methodist minister, maintains in the following viewpoint that the high levels of gun ownership in America are very much responsible for the relatively high levels of violent crime in the United States. Rates of firearms homicide are higher where guns are more plentiful, he argues. Therefore, laws that reduce gun availability and restrict gun ownership will reduce violent crime. Burton points to the 1993 Brady Bill as a law that has successfully reduced gun availability and asserts that the public supports further gun control legislation.

As you read, consider the following questions:
1. What is the author's view of state gun control laws?
2. What does Burton say is unique about the United States among other industrialized nations?
3. How many handgun purchases has the Brady Bill prevented since 1993, according to Burton?

Reprinted, with permission, from C. Emory Burton, "The Urgency of Handgun Control," *Christian Social Action*, November/December 1999. (Endnotes in the original have been omitted in this reprint.)

On September 15, a gunman, with no previous criminal record, opened fire with a handgun during a prayer service at the Wedgewood Baptist Church in Fort Worth, Texas, killing seven people, injuring seven others—some critically—and finally taking his own life.

This is only one of several recent incidents involving violence with guns: Columbine High School in Littleton, Colorado; a Jewish community center in Los Angeles; day trading offices in Atlanta; a high school in Georgia. As tragic as these stories are, the sad truth is that firearms kill some 35,000 people every year in the United States, in addition to some 200,000 injuries, many of them serious or disabling.

In 1995, 181 children under the age of 15 were shot and killed in gun-related accidents, according to the National Center for Health Statistics. Hospital emergency rooms treat almost 100,000 Americans each year for gun-related injuries. According to an article in *The Journal of the American Medical Association*, gunshot wounds cost the nation $2.3 billion a year in medical treatment, and almost half of that is paid for with taxpayer's dollars.

Violence in America, first and foremost, is by gun. Two out of every three homicides, about half of all suicides, over one-third of all robberies, and one out of five aggravated assaults are committed with a gun, usually a handgun.

There are some 25 million handguns in this country. More people are killed and maimed with guns in the United States than in any other major country of the world. In fact, the US may well have more gun deaths each year than all other industrialized countries combined.

The figures cited comprise convincing evidence that the proliferation of handguns and their misuse are serious national problems. In spite of the bumper sticker's claim, guns *do* kill people, and they do it at an increasing rate throughout the country. A clear relationship between firearms and violent death and crime has been found.

History and Habit

The United States has come to rely on the gun because of history and habit. Our culture encourages a casual attitude toward firearms, and we have a heritage of the armed, self-reliant citizen. The hero of American movies and TV is the man with a gun. Accustomed to firearms, entertained by drama that portray the gun as a glamorous instrument of personal justice, many Americans underestimate the consequences of widespread firearms availability.

In the days of the frontier, many believed the gun was indispensable simply for survival. We no longer live in such times. Today's increased urbanization and interdependence of American society call for a new approach to firearms. If we do not control guns we will continue to suffer the violence they generate, the crime they cause and the injury they inflict.

Most authorities agree that the handgun is the weapon of concern. The revolver and the pistol are the weapons predominantly used in violent crimes. Although only about one-third of the firearms in the nation are handguns, they account for over 75 percent of all armed violence in the United States. Because the handgun is *concealable* it is the major weapon of crime; because it is *available*, it is the instrument used in suicides and crimes of passion.

The majority of authorities claim that the increase in the number of homicides results in part from the increased use of firearms. The accessibility of guns (domestic manufacture of handguns has risen in the last several years) contributes significantly to the number of unpremeditated homicides and to the seriousness of many assaults.

When the number of handguns increases, gun violence increases; where there are fewer guns, there is less gun violence. *A policy that reduces the availability of handguns will reduce the amount of firearms violence*. When attention is focused not on the number of crimes committed but on the proportion of crimes involving guns, an inference can be drawn that control systems that substantially reduce the number of guns are effective in reducing the level of gun violence.

Will Gun Control Work?

But the root causes of US violence go much deeper than gun ownership and the question remains: Will strict gun control significantly reduce killings and injuries caused by guns? The evidence seems overwhelming that it would. Curbing the available instruments will reduce the fatalities caused by

criminals, even if the motivational and the structural predis-
positions to engage in crime would remain untouched.

A number of studies confirm that the proportion of gun use
in violence rises and falls with gun ownership. An important
point is that in areas where gun ownership is high, both the
percent of murders committed by guns, and the general murder rate, are high. In general, states with a high ownership of
guns have a higher percentage of homicides using firearms.

Rob Rogers. Reprinted with permission from United Feature Syndicate.
All rights reserved.

The simple fact is that murder and other crimes committed with firearms occur more frequently where guns are
most plentiful and gun control laws least stringent. This applies both to the overall murder rate and to the percentage
of murders involving firearms.

A more telling point is that, with two or three exceptions,
states do not presently have effective gun legislation. Many
of the laws are obsolete, unenforced, or unenforceable. Guns
are readily in the grasp of psychotics, incompetents, alco-
holics, criminals—nearly anyone who wants them. Major
problems result when guns are brought in to a state from the
outside and circumvent that state's relatively strict laws. This
frustrates efforts at state and local regulation. A good case

can be made for replacing our haphazard, poorly enforced, ineffectual state and local laws with stringent and comprehensive federal legislation. The enactment of strong federal limitations is a prerequisite to success of local measures.

A Global Perspective

The United States is the only nation in the industrialized world that permits the almost unlimited private ownership of guns. Not unexpectedly, the accidental death rates in most other countries are much below those in the United States. Firearms death per 100,000 people (1992–94 data) show: The United States, 15.22; Finland, 6.86; France, 6.35; Australia, 2.94; England and Wales, .46; and Japan, .07. More people are killed in gun homicides in one day in the United States than in an entire year in Japan.

A Handgun for Defense

One argument in defense of handguns is that they are needed by the average citizen for protection, especially against burglars. However, a gun is rarely an effective means of protecting the home. The gun-toting homeowner is more likely to get shot than the intruder. It has been estimated that for every burglar stopped by a gun, four to six homeowners or family members are killed accidentally by a gun. About .2 percent of home burglaries result in the firearms death or injury of the intruder by the householder. Furthermore, keeping a gun at home only offers thieves one more item to steal. At least 150,000 guns are stolen every year, most of them handguns.

A popular defense in the argument against gun control is that the Second Amendment guarantees the individual's rights to "keep and bear arms." The initial intent of the Second Amendment was to forbid Congress from prohibiting the maintenance of a state militia. The Supreme Court has ruled five times that the Second Amendment is limited to service by citizens in state militias.

What People Want

One of the ironies of American politics is that there is no meaningful national gun control legislation despite the support by sizable majorities for stricter gun controls. A recent Harris Poll found that 69 percent of the public, and 57 percent of gun owners, want stricter gun control laws. In a CBS News poll, two-thirds of the public said Congress should pass stricter gun control laws, and the same percentage would favor registering all firearms. Eighty percent of gun owners favor a three-day waiting period.

The National Rifle Association has successfully opposed most legislative controls over firearms. However the gun lobby is not the omnipotent, monolithic force it is sometimes thought to be. It's membership, 3.5 million a few years ago, is now down to less than three million. There is evidence of a growing number of handgun control organizations at the state and local levels that could eventually lead to meaningful legislation.

Organizations such as Handgun Control Inc. are working to influence the national scene. The Brady Bill has prevented as many as 250,000 handgun purchases since its passage in 1993. By targeting both the supply and demand for guns, the city of Boston went more than two years without a single young person dying from gunshot wounds. Enforcing a law against possessing both guns and drugs, the city of Richmond seized 512 guns and sent 215 violators to jail; homicide and robbery rates went down 30 percent. It is now illegal to sell guns and ammunition in Los Angeles County. Lawsuits against the gun industry claim they lack safety devices in their products, and make it too easy for criminals and juveniles to obtain guns. Most mainline professional police associations, and almost all major medical associations, now favor more effective gun control.

At the very least, ownership and possession of all handguns should be restricted to those who meet certain eligibility requirements, who can establish a clear need for the weapon, and can demonstrate their competence in using guns. Ownership of every gun would be registered, just as ownership of every automobile is now registered. The background of each applicant would be investigated, a photograph and fingerprints taken, and a test administered to determine the applicant's knowledge of handgun use and storage safety. Such a standard of restrictive licensing, as recommended by presidential commissions on violence, would reduce substantially the handguns now in civilian hands.

The Time Has Come

Of course effective handgun legislation would take some effort, as would any constructive social proposal, but it would be less costly than some have indicated. The focus is on handguns, which comprise only 35 percent of all guns. The cost per application under restrictive licensing may be offset by the smaller number of applications generated. While an excellent case can be made for banning handguns altogether (with some exceptions like the police and security guards), it would not mean that existing handguns would be confiscated. And it would not affect rifles or shotguns.

The United States pays a terrible price for its heritage of guns. They have scarred our national character, marking many of the most terrible moments of our history. Guns bloody the present and imperil the future. The time has come to come to grips with this national menace once and for all. To allow gun ownership to increase unchecked would mean a continued and greater loss of lives.

No other form of personal violence reflects the national negligence that has allowed the misuse of this powerful weapon to escalate so far. The price for not taking strong effective action is more than our cities and our society should have to bear, and it would not be honoring the Christ who came that we might have life and have it more abundantly.

| "Scholarly analysis of decades of firearm-
related data and research consistently
demonstrates that guns do not cause crime."

Gun Ownership Does Not Contribute to Violent Crime

Glen Otero

Glen Otero is an adjunct fellow at the Claremont Institute, a libertarian think thank in California. In the viewpoint that follows, he argues that the relationship between gun owner-ship and violent crime is not as clear-cut as gun control ad-vocates often claim. Otero refutes several "myths" about guns and crime, such as the idea that gun availability con-tributes to crime, that other countries have lower crime rates because of gun control laws, and that few people use guns for self-defense. Finally, Otero disputes the evidence that gun control laws will reduce crime and concludes that antigun advocates have seriously misled the public on this issue.

As you read, consider the following questions:
1. What was the conclusion of the 1978 National Institute of Justice study that the author describes?
2. What is significant about the fact that rates for both gun homicide and non-gun homicide are lower in the United Kingdom than in the United States, in Otero's opinion?
3. About how many defensive gun uses were there per year from 1988 to 1993, according to the study cited by Otero?

Excerpted from Glen Otero, "Ten Myths About Gun Control," a publication of the Claremont Institute, at www.claremont.org/gsp/gsp60.cfm. Reprinted by permission of the Claremont Institute.

M*yth: The proliferation of guns in this country is responsible for an increase in the violent crime rate.*

This is arguably the most pervasive untruth associated with firearms. It is true that there is a great deal of gun-related violent crime in this country, including homicide, robbery and assault. Additionally, the proliferation of firearms in this country has been steadily increasing. These two facts have led many to believe that the increase in guns in this country is responsible for the increase in violent crime. However, decades of data collecting and analysis reveal that nothing about a guns/crime relationship is self-evident.

In 1978 the National Institute of Justice initiated a study to examine the relationship between firearms and violence. Upon reviewing the criminological research to date, the authors of the study concluded that there were no strong causal connections between private gun ownership and the crime rate. Furthermore, they added that there was no good evidence supporting the idea that homicide occurs just because guns are readily available, or its corollary, that many homicides would not occur were guns less available.

Since 1978, criminological studies examining the relationship between violent crime and private gun ownership have typically found no significant positive effect of gun ownership on the violent crime rate. Some studies actually find a negative relationship. In other words, areas with high gun ownership experienced less crime than comparable areas with lower firearm ownership. Studies that draw a causal inference from a gun/homicide correlation usually fail to take into account the possible reverse relationship. That is, these studies do not address the possibility that high crime rates may have stimulated higher gun ownership, and not just the reverse.

The national homicide, gun homicide, robbery and gun robbery rates, as well as the percentage of guns involved in aggravated assault, have not significantly increased from what they were in 1974. However, the number of firearms in this country increased 75 percent between 1974–1994, for a total of nearly 236 million guns. While the number of guns steadily increased in this country between 1974–1994, half of that time the homicide and robbery rates were decreasing, the other half they were increasing, resulting in no net change. The proliferation of firearms during this period cannot be held responsible for an increase in the violent crime rate when in fact there has been no such increase. Furthermore, since 1994, the homicide rate has continued to drop, hitting a low in 1996 not seen since 1969. . . .

International Comparisons

Myth: Strict gun control laws have been successful in lowering crime in the UK and Canada.

Comparing the U.S. to the low guns/low crime societies of the United Kingdom or Canada is one of the most common arguments among gun control advocates. In rebuttal, gun control opponents typically reference high guns/low crime nations such as Switzerland and Israel. However, these comparisons miss the mark. The futility of pairwise comparisons between nations' crime rates relative to their gun ownership becomes apparent once one realizes that there are countries with every permutation: the U.S. (high guns/high crime); Switzerland and Israel (high guns/low crime); Japan (low guns/low crime); and Mexico (low guns/high crime). Any two countries can be compared or contrasted to make any point desired. . . .

Gun control advocates claim that the crime rate is low in the UK because the British have fewer guns than Americans. But European countries have always had lower violent crime rates than the U.S., even before strict gun control laws were passed. Moreover, many violent crime rates in Europe and elsewhere are increasing faster than in the U.S. right now.

Furthermore, the logic of the low guns/low crime rate fails when one considers that the UK's homicide rate is lower for non-gun homicides as well. Clearly, fewer homicides committed with knives, sticks, etc. cannot be attributable to gun control. . . .

To summarize, there is no consistent global correlation between gun availability and violent crime rates.

Guns for Self-Defense

Myth: Few people actually use guns for self-defense.

The National Crime Victimization Survey (NCVS) predicted in 1987 that 83 percent of people in this country

54

would be a victim of violent crime during their lifetime. Considering the violent crime rate has not changed significantly, about 80 percent of the citizenry, in possession of over 230 million guns, with nearly half the households having a gun, are going to come face to face with a violent criminal one day. This situation makes one think that there would be many instances of defensive gun use in this country. In fact, thirteen studies conducted between 1976 and 1994 estimated that there were between 770,00 and 3.6 million civilian defensive gun uses per year.

Reprinted by permission of Chuck Asay and Creators Syndicate. © 1999 Creators Syndicate, Inc.

The National Self-Defense Survey (NSDS), conducted by Gary Kleck and Marc Gertz in 1993, has yielded the most accurate estimate of defensive gun use to date. While designing this landmark study, the authors corrected many flaws found in several previous surveys. In doing so, the authors constructed the first survey ever specifically designed to tally the number of defensive gun uses in this country. The survey revealed that between 1988-1993 civilians used guns in self-defense 2.2-2.5 million times per year, saving between 240,000-400,000 lives each year. Based on their results, Kleck and Gertz estimated that the number of defensive gun uses is three to four times that of illegal gun uses. . . .

Gun Control Is Not the Answer

Myth: Gun control laws take guns out of the hands of criminals and lower violent crime.

Gun control as a whole has not worked to reduce violent crime rates in this country. A large amount of the research on gun control measures, particularly that referenced by gun control advocacy groups, is technically poor. Out of the 21 most accurate studies, 17 found that gun control laws did not reduce violent crime rates; two studies resulted in ambiguous results and two studies indicated a negative (inverse) effect on violent crime rates. Furthermore, of the 21 studies, the most comprehensive one tested the effects of 19 different gun control laws on six categories of violent crime. The researchers found that of 102 direct tests, only three demonstrated definitively that a particular measure worked in reducing the rate of a particular violent crime. Fifteen tests yielded ambiguous results; the remaining 84 tests yielded negative results. The authors concluded that the various gun control laws have no overall significant effect on violent crime rates. Summarily, the body of research on the effects of gun control laws cannot be considered supportive of their efficacy.

A gun control law that has spawned a lot of controversy is the Brady Handgun Violence Prevention Act or Brady Bill. The Brady law requires a mandatory five-day waiting period between the purchase and acquisition of a handgun from a federally licensed dealer. During this waiting period it is determined whether the prospective purchaser of a handgun is a person prohibited ownership of handguns by any State or Federal law. Despite research demonstrating that waiting periods do not lower violent crime (see above), the Brady Act went into effect on February 28, 1994.

When the Brady Bill was signed into law, eighteen states and Washington D.C. were automatically exempt from the law because they already had stricter gun control laws. These exempt states and D.C. accounted for 63 percent of the nation's violent crimes and 58 percent of the nation's murders. Two of the originally exempt states, California and

New York, have the highest and second highest number of murders and violent crimes, respectively. By 1997, ten more states had become exempt from the Brady Bill. The 28 exempt states and D.C. accounted for 75 percent of all violent crimes and 70 percent of the murders in the nation. In fact, California and New York have more violent crimes than the remaining 22 states subject to the five-day wait.

The Clinton Administration is constantly misquoting the Bureau of Justice Statistics regarding the number of persons denied handgun purchases under Brady. The numbers compiled by the Bureau of Justice Statistics need to be viewed with skepticism, since they often do not take into account states that have become exempt under Brady. Despite the number of persons claimed by the President to have been denied handgun purchases under Brady, the actual number is 3 percent, or less, of prospective owners per year. This means that 97 percent of persons attempting to purchase handguns from federally licensed dealers are law-abiding citizens. The actual number is undoubtedly higher since a study conducted by the General Accounting Office (GAO) determined that half of the denials in the first year of Brady enforcement were wrongly dispensed due to clerical errors and other technicalities, and later reversed.

Using crime rate data for all 3,054 counties in the U.S. between 1977 and 1994, John Lott completed an analysis of the Brady law's impact during its first year. His research demonstrated that the law had no significant effect on murder or robbery rates, while rape and aggravated assault rates experienced significant increases.

The GAO also determined that in the first 17 months of Brady enforcement, only seven individuals were convicted of illegal attempts to purchase a handgun, and only three of these were sent to prison. . . .

Antigun Bias in the Media

Scholarly analysis of decades of firearm-related data and research consistently demonstrates that guns do not cause crime. Yet, many Americans have a different opinion. How does such a gap between the truth in gun ownership and public opinion arise?

MediaWatch, a media watchdog organization, examined every gun control policy story on four evening shows (ABC's *World News Tonight*, *CBS Evening News*, CNN's *The World Today*, and *NBC Nightly News*) and three morning broadcasts (ABC's *Good Morning America*, *CBS This Morning*, and NBC's *Today*) between July 1, 1995 and June 30, 1997. MediaWatch calculated that in those two years 157 pro-gun control stories were aired compared to 10 stories opposed to gun control, while another 77 stories were neutral. This approximate 16:1 ratio in favor of gun control hardly depicts an unbiased media. Therein lies a major obstacle to spreading the truth about gun ownership. While adopting a decidedly biased anti-gun stance, the media also fails to promote firearm safety and education.

And judging from the depth and breadth of gun related myths in circulation, a firearm education is one thing this country desperately needs . . . and deserves.

> *"Sensible gun laws have a role to play in our criminal justice system. That includes allowing law-abiding adults to carry firearms."*

Legalizing Concealed Weapons Makes Society Safer

Don B. Kates

Don B. Kates is a criminological policy analyst with the Pacific Research Institute in San Francisco and the co-author, with Gary Gleck, of *The Great American Gun War: Essays in Firearms and Violence*. In the following viewpoint, Kates argues that allowing ordinary citizens to carry their guns in public deters crime. He points to incidents in which potential shooting sprees were stopped by armed civilians as well as to studies showing that violent crime rates have gone down in states that permit "concealed-carry," as the policy is known. Rather than restricting gun ownership among ordinary people, Kates concludes, the government should permit law-abiding citizens to carry firearms.

As you read, consider the following questions:
1. How does the author describe Israel's "different approach" to crime control?
2. How was the October 1997 school shooting in Pearl, Mississippi, ended, according to Kates?
3. What are the conclusions of researchers John Lott and David Mustard, as cited by Kates?

Reprinted, with permission, from Don B. Kates, "Making a Case for Gun Ownership: Israeli-U.S. Contrasts," *The Christian Science Monitor*, December 16, 1997.

When a 14-year-old high school student shot eight people, killing three, during a Paducah, Kentucky, prayer meeting not long ago, many good-hearted, liberal people saw only one possible response: Tighten gun laws even further, or outlaw and confiscate guns altogether.

Experience shows, however, that gun laws are not much use. Over the past 20 years, handgun ownership has doubled, while the number of homicides has markedly declined.

Virtually without exception, ordinary law-abiding people do not murder. Our laws already prohibit guns to those who do murder—felons, drug addicts, juveniles, and the deranged—but they manage to kill anyway.

Israel's Example

Israel, which has much more experience with massacres, has a different approach. It licenses trained, responsible adults so that armed civilians will be ready and able to defend themselves (and others) in public places.

Israeli criminologist Abraham Tennenbaum says, "The homicide rate in Israel has always been very low—much lower than in the United States . . . despite the greater availability of guns to law-abiding civilians." In contrast, laws in California and New York make it virtually impossible for anyone lacking special influence to obtain a license to carry a concealed handgun.

Consider some examples of how these contrasting policies work:

• On April 3, 1984, three Arab terrorists trying to machine-gun a Jerusalem crowd killed only one victim before being shot down by Israeli civilians. The next day, the surviving terrorist said his group had planned to gun down other crowds of shoppers, leaving before police could arrive. They had not known that Israeli civilians were armed.

• On July 18, 1984, an unemployed security guard shot 31 unarmed adults and children in a San Ysidro, California, McDonald's, before being killed by a police sniper 77 minutes after the tragedy began.

• On April 6, 1994, (quoting an Associated Press release from Jerusalem): "A Palestinian opened fire with a submachine gun at a bus stop near the port of Ashdod today, killing one Israeli and wounding four before being shot to death by bystanders, officials said. . . ."

• Four months earlier, Colin Ferguson shot down 22 unarmed victims on the Long Island Railroad, killing five.

John Lott's Research on Concealed-Carry Laws

My colleague William Landes and I have compiled data on all the multiple-victim public shootings that took place in the United States from 1977 to 1995. We included incidents where at least two people were killed or injured in a public place; and to focus on the type of shooting seen in the Colorado rampage, we excluded gang wars or shootings that were the byproduct of another crime, such as robbery. The U.S. averaged 21 such shootings annually, with an average of 1.8 people killed and 2.7 wounded in each one.

We examined a range of different policies, including sentencing laws and gun laws (such as waiting periods), to see what might stop or deter these killings. We found that higher arrest and conviction rates, longer prison sentences, and the death penalty reduce murders generally. But neither the gun laws nor the frequency or severity of punishment turned out to have any significant effect on public shootings.

We found only one policy that does have such an effect: letting adults without criminal records or a history of significant mental illness carry concealed handguns. The impact of these "right to carry" laws, now on the books in 31 states, has been dramatic. During the 19 years covered in our study, states that passed such laws saw the number of multiple-victim public shootings decline by an average of 84 percent. Deaths from these shootings plummeted on average by 90 percent, injuries by 82 percent. To the extent that attacks still occur in states that have enacted these laws, they disproportionately occur in those areas in which concealed handguns are forbidden.

John Lott Jr., "Gun Show: Why New Gun Laws Won't Work," *National Review*, May 31, 1999.

• On Oct. 9, 1997, in Pearl, Mississippi, a 16-year-old stabbed his mother to death and shot nine people at his high school, killing two. His rampage ended when the assistant principal, carrying a .45 semi-automatic pistol, confronted the boy.

According to Florida State University criminologist Gary

Kleck, who co-authored a book on the subject of guns and violence with me, there are some 2.5 million incidents annually where law-abiding, responsible Americans use handguns to stop crimes.

Handgun Control Inc. tells prospective victims never to resist rape or robbery in any way: "The best defense against injury is to put up no defense—give them what they want or run." But Professor Kleck says victims who use firearms to repel criminals are only half as likely to be injured as victims who submit—and much less likely to be raped or robbed.

Mississippi and 30 other states allow responsible adults to carry guns. The results were evaluated by the University of Chicago's John Lott and David Mustard, based on statistics from all 3,054 counties in the nation since 1977. Professors Lott and Mustard concluded that in states with these new laws, thousands of murders, rapes, and robberies were averted. In a forthcoming paper, Professor Lott also found that the number of massacre-type homicides have steadily declined in states adopting the new laws but continue unabated in California, New York, and other states that have rejected them.

Don't Disarm Law-Abiding Citizens

Many antigun newspapers do not find such studies (or the Israeli incidents) "fit to print." Rather, they editorialize that indiscriminately banning guns to the general citizenry would reduce both massacres and ordinary murders. Yet, in more candid moments, even antigun advocates admit laws can't disarm terrorists or homicidal maniacs.

Carefully tailored, sensible gun laws have a role to play in our criminal justice system. That includes allowing law-abiding adults to carry firearms. Banning responsible, law abiding citizens from owning guns will not work. Crime can't be curbed by disarming its victims.

"Contrary to the gun lobby's claim, no evidence exists to suggest that 'an armed society is a polite society.'"

Legalizing Concealed Weapons Does Not Make Society Safer

Douglas Weil

Douglas Weil is research director at the Center to Prevent Handgun Violence, an organization that works to reduce gun violence through research, advocacy, and education. In the following viewpoint, he argues that laws that allow civilians to carry concealed weapons endanger the public. Under these laws, writes Weil, the only requirement for a concealed-carry permit is that the applicant has not been convicted of a violent crime. This system, he asserts, enables many ill-tempered, poorly trained, and unstable people to carry guns. Weil points to examples of violent incidents involving concealed-carry permit holders. Finally, he argues that studies linking concealed-carry laws to reduced crime are groundless.

As you read, consider the following questions:
1. What is wrong with Texas's background check system for applicants who want to carry concealed weapons, in the author's opinion?
2. How do law enforcement officials view concealed-carry laws, according to Weil?
3. What have critics said of John Lott's studies on the effects of concealed-carry laws, as quoted by Weil?

Reprinted from Douglas Weil, "Carrying Concealed Guns Is Not the Solution," *IntellectualCapital.com*, March 26, 1998, by permission of the author.

Why should you worry about more people carrying concealed handguns?

On September 10, 1997, five men licensed to carry concealed handguns got into a fight outside a Pittsburgh saloon after exchanging "hostile looks." All of the men fired their weapons and ended up in the hospital.

Earlier this year in Indianapolis, two women were unintentionally shot when a concealed handgun fell out of a man's pocket at a crowded Planet Hollywood restaurant.

In February 1997, two Tulsa men were arguing over who would take their four-year-old granddaughter home from day care. One of the men, who had a permit to carry a concealed weapon, shot the other man in front of 250 school children.

A Background Check of What?

Why were these dangerous and poorly-trained people allowed to carry concealed handguns? They live in states that recently weakened "carrying concealed weapons" (CCW) laws.

This legislation—a favorite of the gun lobby—takes discretion away from law enforcement in determining who receives a concealed weapons license and requires the state to allow virtually anyone who is not a convicted felon to carry a loaded handgun. Under this system, the background check required of applicants for CCW licenses is supposed to screen out people with violent criminal histories, but it cannot screen out all criminals or people with bad tempers or bad judgment—and no one should think otherwise.

Daniel Blackman is one example of a dangerous man who was allowed to carry a concealed weapon despite prior criminal behavior. In February 1996, the former candidate for judge in Broward County, Florida, threatened to put three bullets in the head of a meter maid who had written him a ticket—behavior that should have prevented him from carrying a concealed handgun but did not. Though he was arrested, Blackman was not convicted of a crime because he agreed to seek psychological treatment. A year later, Blackman was arrested again, this time for pulling a gun on an emergency-room doctor who refused to write him a prescription. Only then was his CCW license revoked.

In states with lax CCW laws, hundreds of licensees have

committed crimes both before and after their licensure. For example, in Texas, which weakened its CCW law in 1996, the Department of Public Safety reported that felony and misdemeanor cases involving CCW permit holders rose 54.4% between 1996 and 1997. Charges filed against Texas CCW holders included kidnapping, sexual assault, aggravated assault with a deadly weapon, illegal drug possession and sales, drunken driving and impersonating a police officer. Clearly, the Texas background check does not ensure that everyone who receives a CCW license is a responsible or upstanding citizen.

Jim Borgman. Reprinted by special permission of King Features Syndicate.

From Texas to Illinois and California to Delaware, law-enforcement officials have led the charge against this dangerous liberalization because they know that more guns will only lead to more violence. Thanks to the efforts of our men and women in blue and concerned citizens, the gun lobby has not passed any new concealed-weapons legislation in more than a year. Despite the opposition of most voters, the gun lobby currently is trying to pass these senseless laws in Michigan and Nebraska, and also has set its sights on Kansas, Ohio and Missouri.

A Lott of Nothing

The gun lobby attempts to justify this dangerous political agenda by citing research conducted by Dr. John Lott. Lott's study concludes that making it easier for citizens to carry concealed weapons reduces violent crime rates. What the gun lobby and Lott do not say is that this study has been totally discredited by many well-respected, independent researchers.

In fact, in a nationally-televised symposium at which Lott's work was critiqued, Dr. Daniel Nagin of Carnegie Mellon University, Dr. Daniel Black of the University of Kentucky, and Dr. Jens Ludwig of Georgetown University agreed that Lott's study is so flawed that "nothing can be learned of it" and that it "cannot be used responsibly to formulate policy." Since then, no credible evidence has been produced to rebut the conclusions of Black, Nagin and Ludwig, or other researchers who have identified additional flaws with Lott's work.

Contrary to the gun lobby's claim, no evidence exists to suggest that "an armed society is a polite society." In reality, the United States already has more guns in civilian hands than any other industrialized nation, and not surprisingly, we also have one of the world's highest rates of gun crime. As the casualties of weak concealed-weapons laws begin to mount, it is unconscionable that Lott and the gun lobby continue to use this flawed data to put more guns on the street.

Fortunately, the American people and law enforcement know better. They deserve primary consideration from their state representatives, not the special-interest gun lobby. It is truly a matter of life and death.

*"Muggers or rapists who are ready to attack
you on the street are likely to have a sudden
change of plans if you pull out a gun."*

Gun Ownership Increases Personal Safety

Thomas Sowell

In the following viewpoint Thomas Sowell, a nationally syndicated columnist, criticizes prominent gun control advocates for ignoring evidence that gun ownership can deter crime and that guns are useful for self-defense. In particular, he denounces celebrities who campaign against guns but also hire armed bodyguards. Sowell argues that law-abiding citizens should own guns because criminals are less likely to attack an armed citizen. He also notes that most of the high-profile shootings exploited by the media have occurred in places where victims are likely to be unarmed, such as schools and churches.

As you read, consider the following questions:

1. In order to have a rational discussion on gun control, what must those on both sides of the debate acknowledge, in Sowell's opinion?
2. What is true of more than 90 percent of all uses of guns in self-defense, according to Sowell?
3. Why are statistics on the number of children killed by guns misleading, in the author's view?

Reprinted from Thomas Sowell, "Firing Gun Control Hypocrisy," *The Washington Times*, June 4, 2000, by permission of Thomas Sowell and Creators Syndicate. © 2000 Creators Syndicate, Inc.

[A ctress and talk show host] Rosie O'Donnell is only the latest liberal to be vociferously in favor of gun control for other people—and yet ready to use firearms for their own protection. Others have included columnist Carl Rowan and Adolph Ochs Sulzberger of the *New York Times*, whose newspaper has been 200 percent behind gun control laws for years.

Rosie O'Donnell has hired a security guard to protect her young son and the guard has applied for a gun permit. However, children of famous people are by no means the only ones at risk. A recent study showed a 15-year-old black youth in the inner city has about 1 chance in 12 of being killed before he reaches age 45.

Gun Control Hypocrisy

Why is it more important for Rosie O'Donnell's son to have armed protection than for a black youth, or other people living in high-crime neighborhoods, to have armed protection? Here is the same "do as I say, not as I do" hypocrisy found among liberals who want to prevent other people from exercising the same school choice that they exercise for their own children.

There will be no rational discussion of gun control until both sides acknowledge that guns both cost lives and save lives, so that the issue boils down to the net effect. This is a factual question and the facts are readily available, so there is no excuse for this to continue to be discussed in terms of assumptions and theories.

The empirical data are very clear. Where ordinary, law-abiding citizens have been allowed to carry firearms, violent crimes—including shootings—have gone down, not up. Where local governments have begun restricting the availability of firearms, including requiring all sorts of "safety" provisions, violent crimes have gone up, even at a time when such crimes are going down nationally.

Obviously, whenever guns are widely available in a country of a quarter of a billion people, somebody somewhere is going to get killed accidentally or by someone whose anger or viciousness gets out of hand. That has to be weighed against the lives that are saved when an armed citizenry reduces violent crime. Taking both these things into account, there has still been a net reduction in violent crime and deaths from allowing law-abiding people ready access to firearms.

This is not a theory. It is what has happened, again and again, in communities all across this country. The facts simply do not fit the gun control advocates' theories.

Guns and Self-Defense

More than 90 percent of all uses of guns in self-defense do not involve actually firing the weapon, despite gun control advocates' assumption that we are all such trigger-happy idiots that letting ordinary citizens have guns will lead to bullets flying hither and yon. Like virtually every other liberal crusade, gun control is based on the assumption that other people lack common sense and must be controlled by the superior wisdom and virtue of the anointed.

Reprinted by permission of Chuck Asay and Creators Syndicate. © 1999 Creators Syndicate, Inc.

But both criminals and law-abiding citizens have common sense. An intruder in your home who hears you loading a shotgun in the next room is going to be out of there before you can get to where he is—and he is very unlikely ever to come back. Muggers or rapists who are ready to attack you on the street are likely to have a sudden change of plans if you pull out a gun.

Every incident where someone opens fire at random in a public place is exploited to the hilt by the media and by gun control advocates. But have you noticed that such shootings occur in places where the potential victims are unlikely to be armed? Restaurants, schools, churches and synagogues are far more likely to be targets than gun shows or conventions of the National Rifle Association. Open fire on people who have firearms themselves and that can be the last dumb thing you do.

Gun Control Lies

The facts are readily available in books like *More Guns, Less Crime* by John Lott or *Pointblank* by Gary Kleck. But gun control advocates do not want to face the facts—not if it means giving up their vision of the world and their sense of superiority, based on that vision. Not even if it costs other people their lives.

When gun control advocates throw around figures about how many children are killed by guns, they don't tell you that most of these "children" are teen-age gangsters, not little kids who find loaded guns around the home. Joseph Schumpeter once said the first thing a man will do for his ideals is lie. Gun control advocates prove his point.

| *"Guns kept in the home for self-protection are more oftentimes used to kill somebody you know than to kill in self-defense."*

Gun Ownership Decreases Personal Safety

Handgun Control Inc.

Handgun Control Inc. (HCI) is an activist organization that supports federal regulation of the manufacture, sale, and civilian possession of handguns and automatic weapons. In the following viewpoint, HCI refutes the idea that gun ownership is an effective means of self-defense. Guns kept in the home are rarely used in self-defense, it argues. HCI notes that keeping a gun in the home increases the risk that an argument or scuffle in the home might end in homicide. Keeping a gun in the home also increases the risks of gun-related accidents, especially if there are children in the home. In HCI's view, the dangers of gun ownership far exceed the benefits.

As you read, consider the following questions:
1. According to FBI statistics, as cited by Handgun Control Inc., how many justifiable homicides were there in 1996, as compared to how many handgun murders?
2. How many people were killed accidentally or unintentionally by firearms in 1996, according to the viewpoint?
3. What are Child Access Prevention laws, as described by HCI?

Reprinted, with permission, from "Guns in the Home," a publication of Handgun Control Inc., at www.handguncontrol.org/facts/ib/gunhome.asp.

There are over 200 million guns in America. That's almost one gun per every man, woman and child in the United States. Guns are not just in urban and rural homes, they're everywhere—cities, towns, suburbs and farms. In fact, there is a gun in 43% of households with children in America. There's a loaded gun in one in every ten households with children, and a gun that's left unlocked and just hidden away in one in every eight family homes.

Guns Are Rarely Used in Self-Defense

Does a gun in the home make you safer? No. Despite claims by the National Rifle Association (NRA) that you need a gun in your home to protect you and your family from possible home invasion, public health research demonstrates that the person most likely to shoot you or a family member with a gun already has the keys to your house. Simply put: guns kept in the home for self-protection are more oftentimes used to kill somebody you know than to kill in self-defense; 22 times more likely, according to a 1998 study by the *New England Journal of Medicine*.

More kids, teenagers and adult family members are dying from firearms in their own home than criminal intruders. When someone is home, a gun is used for protection in fewer than two percent of home invasion crimes. You may be surprised to know that, in 1996, according to the FBI, there were only 176 justifiable handgun homicides compared with a total of 9,390 handgun murders in the United States.

Once a bullet leaves a gun, who is to say that it will stop only a criminal and not a family member? Yet at every opportunity the National Rifle Association uses the fear of crime to promote the need for ordinary citizens to keep guns in their home for self-protection.

Keeping a Gun in the Home Can Be Deadly

Because handguns and other firearms are so easily accessible to many children, adolescents and other family members in their homes, the risks of gun violence in the home increase dramatically. Consider this: The risk of homicide in the home is three times greater in households with guns. The risk of suicide is five times greater in households with guns.

What's more, tragic stories of accidental or unintentional shootings from the careless storage of guns at home are all too common.

National Trends, Local Tragedies

A Gun in the Home: Key Facts

- When a gun is present in the home, a marital or sibling dispute can quickly erupt into a homicide. According to a 1994 Bureau of Justice Statistics report, victims in spousal murders were the most likely to have died from gunshot wounds (53%), compared to victims in other types of family murder. In 1996, 13,788 people were killed using firearms and thousands more were seriously injured.
- Guns are also the weapon of choice for troubled individuals who commit suicide. In 1996, firearms were used in 18,166 suicide deaths in America. Among young people, youths aged 10–19 committed suicide with a gun every six hours. That's over 1,300 young people in a single year.
- A gun in the home also increases the likelihood of an unintentional shooting, particularly among children. Unintentional shootings commonly occur when children find an adult's loaded handgun in a drawer or closet, and while playing with it shoot themselves, a sibling or a friend. In 1996, 1,134 people—many of them children—were killed accidentally or unintentionally by firearms.

When Tragedy Strikes Home: Recent Incidents

- Recently, tragedy unexpectedly struck a home in Pontiac, Michigan. On July 15, 1999, a two-year-old boy was killed as he and his three-year-old brother played with a gun in their bedroom with their seven-month-old sister nearby.
- On July 21, 1999, in Lakepark, Florida, a six-year-old boy fatally shot his five-year-old brother, Corey Andrew Wilson, as the boys played with a shotgun they found under a bed in their grandparents' bedroom.
- Shawn Adam Miller, a sixteen-year-old boy from Travis County, Texas, described by neighbors as a "happy-go-lucky" teenager, shot and killed his parents, a 13-year-old neighbor and then himself in his home on July 20,

Are Handguns Useful for Self-Defense?

Guns are rarely useful for self-defense. A handgun only increases one's risk of death and injury and creates a false sense of security. Even police officers, who are trained in handling weapons, are at risk of having their gun used against them. A study published in the *American Journal of Public Health* found that twenty percent of police officers shot and killed in the last 15 years were killed with their own firearms. Research also shows that the use of a firearm to resist a violent assault actually increases the victim's risk of injury and death.

Educational Fund to End Handgun Violence, "6th Annual Citizens' Conference to Stop Handgun Violence: Conference Briefing Book," October 1999, www.csgv.org/content/resources/resc_briefbook.html.

1999. Shawn used a .410-gauge shotgun owned by his family and kept in their home.

- On May 3, 1999, in Chicago, Illinois, a 16-year-old boy unintentionally killed his 15-year-old cousin while playing with a .38-caliber Smith & Wesson handgun. The two boys were visiting their grandmother's apartment, when they started playing with the loaded gun which accidentally discharged.

Children at Risk

Do parents do a good job of keeping kids away from guns in the home? No. A recent study by Peter Hart Research on behalf of the Center to Prevent Handgun Violence found that, even though most parents realize that guns in the home endanger their children, many parents still leave guns accessible to kids. Specifically, in the survey of 806 parents, 43% of households with children have guns, and 23% of gun households keep a gun loaded. 28% keep a gun hidden and unlocked. 54% of parents said that they would be highly concerned about their child's safety if they knew there was a gun in the home of their child's friend. Despite many parents' concern about the immediate dangers that guns left in the house pose to their children, they are failing to take the necessary steps to help ensure their children's safety. Many parents, though, do not see guns as a personal threat to their children or their family at all.

Too often a parent drops off their child at a friend's house for an afternoon play session or a sleep-over party not know-ing that the car ride would be the last time they would see their child alive. Why? The study found that most parents don't discuss the issue of guns in the home with the parents of their children's friends. Amazingly, only 30% have asked the parents of their children's friends if there is a gun in the home before allowing a visit. 61% of the parents included in the survey responded that they never even thought about asking other parents about gun accessibility. Clearly, parents don't think about the tragic possibilities of an innocent visit to another home. While parents are asking each other about supervision, food allergies, adult television access, they are ignoring guns—the one factor that could mean the life or death of their child.

Child Access Prevention Laws

Handgun Control supports Child Access Prevention (CAP) laws, or "safe storage" laws that require adults to either store loaded guns in a place that is reasonably inaccessible to children, or if [they're] left out in the open, to use a safety device to lock the gun. If a child obtains an improperly stored, loaded gun, the adult owner is criminally liable.

Although the primary intention of CAP laws is to help prevent unintentional injury, CAP laws also serve to reduce juvenile suicide and homicide by keeping guns out of the reach of children. Currently, 17 states—California, Connecticut, Delaware, Florida, Hawaii, Illinois, Iowa, Maryland, Massachusetts, Minnesota, Nevada, New Jersey, North Carolina, Rhode Island, Texas, Virginia and Wisconsin have enacted CAP laws.

Periodical Bibliography

The following articles have been selected to supplement the diverse views presented in this chapter. Addresses are provided for periodicals not indexed in the *Readers' Guide to Periodical Literature*, the *Alternative Press Index*, the *Social Sciences Index*, or the *Index to Legal Periodicals and Books*.

Jane E. Brody	"In Repeated Studies, Guns Turn Out to Be 'Protection' That Puts Families at Risk," *New York Times*, May 21, 1997.
Angie Cannon	"Missouri Showdown: Vote Against Right to Carry Concealed Guns," *U.S. News & World Report*, April 19, 1999.
Frederick V. Guterl	"Gunslinging in America: Does a Gun Make You Safer or Increase Your Likelihood of Violent Death?" *Discover*, May 1996.
Bronwyn Jones	"Arming Myself with a Gun Is Not the Answer," *Newsweek*, May 22, 2000.
John R. Lott Jr.	"One Case for Guns: Dramatic Cases of Guns Used for Self-Defense Go Unreported," *Christian Science Monitor*, August 21, 2000.
John R. Lott Jr.	"Gun Show: Why New Gun Laws Won't Work," *National Review*, May 31, 1999.
Mother Jones	"Who We Kill," March/April 1996.
New York Times	"Guns and Responsibility: Needed Safety Measures in the Wake of Jonesboro, Ark. Shootings," March 27, 1998.
Romesh Ratnesar	"Should You Carry a Gun?" *Time*, July 6, 1998.
Steven Schnur	"Guns Are Designed to Kill and They Do; By Allowing Their Manufacture and Use We Condone Death," *Christian Science Monitor*, June 17, 1999.
Jacob Sullum and Michael W. Lynch	"Cold Comfort," *Reason*, January 2000.
Jeffery R. Snyder	"Easing Handgun Licenses: Helping the Public Fight Back," *USA Today*, September 1998.

CHAPTER 3

Does the Constitution Protect Private Gun Ownership?

Chapter Preface

Most gun control advocates believe that the surest way to re-duce gun violence in America is to ban or restrict the private ownership of firearms, particularly handguns. Opponents of gun control often claim that banning handguns would be unconstitutional—specifically, that it would violate the Sec-ond Amendment, which protects "the right of the people to keep and bear arms."

While gun control and gun rights advocates have hotly debated the meaning of the Second Amendment for decades, in practice, constitutional concerns have not posed a major obstacle to gun control legislation. The federal gov-ernment and all fifty states have passed numerous laws reg-ulating who may own and carry firearms and what types of weapons should be legal or illegal. Gun control advocates say this is because the framers of the Constitution never in-tended for the Second Amendment to be an obstacle to gun firearms laws. "The right to keep and bear arms as stated in the Constitution is fundamentally based on states' need for a well-regulated militia," states the Educational Fund to End Handgun Violence, "It does not guarantee an individual's right to own firearms for self defense."

However, in a 1996 *Atlantic Monthly* article, lawyer and social critic Wendy Kaminer suggests that this view has had the unintended effect of fueling opposition to even modest gun regulations. "The majority of gun owners," she writes, "would be amenable to gun controls . . . if they didn't per-ceive them as preludes to prohibition." She proposes that the Second Amendment be treated like the First Amend-ment right to free speech: Individuals have a right to free speech, but that speech is still subject to laws against libel, perjury, and copyright infringement. Kaminer reasons that an individual's right to own guns would still be subject to reasonable limits and regulations. "Acknowledging an indi-vidual right to bear arms might facilitate gun control more than denying it ever could," she concludes.

The authors in the following chapter offer their views on the Second Amendment and whether or not it protects an individual's right to own guns.

| "The Second Amendment protects the same
'people' as the other rights guaranteed in
the Bill of Rights; namely you and me."

The Second Amendment Protects Private Gun Ownership

Stefan B. Tahmassebi

Stefan B. Tahmassebi argues in the following viewpoint that the Second Amendment protects individual gun ownership. He notes that because the amendment refers both to a "well-regulated militia" and to "the right of the people to keep and bear arms," many gun control advocates have interpreted the amendment as applying only to state militias rather than individuals. Tahmassebi maintains that this interpretation is simply incorrect. For example, he points to Supreme Court decisions in which the term "militia" has been taken to mean "all citizens capable of bearing arms," and others in which it was recognized that the Second Amendment applies to individuals who do not serve in the armed forces. Tahmassebi is deputy general counsel for the National Rifle Association.

As you read, consider the following questions:
1. What is significant about the case of *Robertson v. Baldwin*, in the author's view?
2. According to Tahmassebi, in *U.S. v. Miller*, the Supreme Court ruled that the Second Amendment protects only what type of firearm?
3. How did the Supreme Court define the term "the people" in the case of *United States v. Verdugo-Urquirdez*, according to the author?

Reprinted from Stefan B. Tahmassebi, "The Second Amendment and the United States Supreme Court," *American Guardian*, May 2000, by permission of the National Rifle Association, © 2000.

Gun prohibitionists often claim that the United States Supreme Court has held that the Second Amendment does not guarantee an individual right to keep and bear arms, but offers only a "collective right" for the organized military forces of the states to have governmentally owned arms. This "Collective Rights" approach is a newcomer to theories of constitutional law and made its first appearance only in the Twentieth Century. Not only does the "Collective Rights" approach run counter to overwhelming textual and historical evidence, but the Supreme Court has never held such a theory applicable to the Second Amendment.

A Fundamental, Individual Right

Dred Scott v. Sandford was the first case in which the Supreme Court mentioned the right to keep and bear arms. The issue before this pre-Civil War and pre-emancipation court was whether blacks were "citizens." The court stated that if blacks were citizens, they would have the same constitutional protections afforded to white citizens, which included the right to keep and bear arms.

"It would give to persons of the negro race . . . the right to enter every other State whenever they pleased, . . . and it would give them the full liberty of speech . . . ; to hold public meetings upon political affairs, and to keep and carry arms wherever they went." The court specifically placed the right to keep and bear arms in the same category as the other fundamental individual rights that are protected from governmental infringement by the Bill of Rights: "Nor can Congress deny to the people the right to keep and bear arms, nor the right to trial by jury, nor compel any one to be a witness against himself in a criminal proceeding."

Nowhere in the opinion does the court suggest that the right to keep and bear arms differs from other fundamental rights and protects only the state government's organized military. Clearly, the court considered the right to keep and bear arms as a fundamental individual right of every "citizen."

United States v. Cruikshank, a post-Civil War and post-emancipation case, arose out of the disarmament and murder of freed blacks in Louisiana (the "Colfax Massacre"). Klansmen were subsequently charged by the federal prosecutor with a conspiracy to prevent blacks from exercising their civil rights, including the right of peaceful assembly and the right to keep and bear arms. The court recognized that the right to peacefully assemble and the right of the people to keep and bear arms were natural rights which even preexisted the Constitution.

The Second Amendment Prohibits Federal Gun Control Laws

The court stated, however, that the First and Second Amendment rights were protections against the federal government only, and did not restrict state government action. The court held that because these fundamental rights existed independently of the Constitution, and because the First and Second Amendments guaranteed only that these rights shall not be infringed by the federal Congress, the federal government had no power to punish a violation of these rights by the Klansmen, who were private individuals. Although the Second Amendment protected a citizen from having his right to keep and bear arms violated by the federal government, the Second Amendment did not protect a citizen from the acts of other private persons.

Clearly, the court considered the right to keep and bear arms (and the right to peaceably assemble) as a fundamental individual civil right of each citizen, which the federal government could not infringe. The court never even suggested that the Second Amendment guaranteed only a state's right to maintain militias rather than an individual citizen's right to keep and bear arms.

Presser v. Illinois involved an Illinois statute which did not prohibit the possession of arms, but merely prohibited "bodies of men to associate together as military organizations, or to drill or parade with arms in cities and towns unless authorized by law. . . ." Presser was indicted for parading a private military unit of 400 armed men through the streets of Chicago without a license. The court concluded that the Illinois statute did not infringe the Second Amendment since the statute did not prohibit the keeping and bearing of arms but rather prohibited the forming of private military organizations and the performance of military exercises in town by groups of armed men without a license to do so. The court found that such prohibitions simply "do not infringe the right of the people to keep and bear arms."

All Citizens Constitute the Militia

The Supreme Court seemed to affirm the holding in *Cruikshank* that the Second Amendment protected individuals only against action by the federal government. However, in the very next paragraph, the court suggests that state governments cannot forbid individuals to keep and bear arms. After stating that "all citizens capable of bearing arms" constitute the "militia," the Court held that the "States cannot . . . prohibit the people from keeping and bearing arms, as so to deprive the United States of their rightful resource for maintaining the public security and disable the people from performing their duty to the general government."

In *Miller v. Texas*, the defendant challenged a Texas statute

---

The Founding Fathers on Gun Ownership

We can only extrapolate and conjecture about how the Founders would have understood the First Amendment's "freedom of the press" to apply to the Playboy Channel, or how the "search and seizure" language of the Fourth Amendment would have been thought to bear on overheard cellular telephone calls. But no ambiguity at all surrounds the attitude of the constitutional generation concerning "the right of the people to keep and bear arms." To put the matter bluntly, the Founders of the United States were what we would nowadays call gun nuts. "One loves to possess arms," Thomas Jefferson wrote to President Washington (whose own gun collection, Don Kates notes, contained more than 50 specimens). . . .

Addressing Virginia's constitutional ratification convention with characteristic exorbitance, Anti-Federalist icon Patrick Henry declared that "the great object is that every man be armed. . . . Everyone who is able may have a gun." And James Madison, author of the Bill of Rights, recognized "the advantage of being armed, which the Americans possess over the people of almost every other nation," whose tyrannical governments are "afraid to trust the people with arms."

Daniel D. Polsby, *Reason*, March 1996.

---

on the bearing of pistols as violative of the Second, Fourth, and Fourteenth Amendments. The problem for Miller was that he failed to timely raise these defenses in the state trial and appellate courts, raising these issues for the first time in the U.S. Supreme Court. While the court held that the Second and Fourth Amendment (prohibiting warrantless searches), of themselves, did not limit state action (as opposed to federal action), the court did not address the defendant's claim that these constitutional protections were made effective against state government action by the Fourteenth Amendment, because Miller did not raise these issues in a timely manner. The Court, thus, left open the possibility that these constitutional rights were made effective against state governments by the Fourteenth Amendment. Lastly, it should be noted that in this case, as in the other Supreme Court cases, the defendant was not a member of the Armed Forces, and yet the Supreme Court did not dismiss Miller's claim on that ground; thus, Miller, as a private citizen, did enjoy individual Second Amendment protection, even if he was not enrolled in the National Guard or Armed Forces.

Robertson v. Baldwin

Robertson v. Baldwin did not involve a Second Amendment claim, but in discussing the 13th Amendment, the Court again recognized the Second Amendment as a "fundamental" individual right of citizens; which, like the other fundamental rights, is not absolute. "The law is perfectly well settled that the first 10 amendments to the Constitution, commonly known as the 'Bill of Rights', were not intended to lay down any novel principles of government, but simply to embody certain guaranties and immunities which we had inherited from our English ancestors, and which had, from time immemorial, been subject to certain well-recognized exceptions, arising from the necessities of the case. . . . Thus, the freedom of speech and of the press (Article 1) does not permit the publication of libels, blasphemous or indecent articles, or other publications injurious to public morals or private reputation; the right of the people to keep and bear arms (Article 2) is not infringed by laws prohibiting the carrying of concealed weapons. . . ."

The reference to state laws that prohibited the carrying of concealed weapons by individuals suggests that the Supreme Court viewed the Second Amendment as being a protection for individual citizens against not only interference by the federal government but also against interference by state governments.

U.S. v. Miller

U.S. v. Miller was the first case in which the Supreme Court addressed a federal firearms statute which was being challenged on Second Amendment grounds. The defendants, who had been charged with interstate transportation of an unregistered sawed off shotgun, challenged the constitutionality of the federal government's National Firearms Act of 1934 ("NFA"). The NFA, a tax statute, did not ban any firearms, but required the registration of, and imposed a $200 transfer tax upon, fully automatic firearms and short barreled rifles and shotguns. The federal trial court held that the NFA violated the defendants' Second Amendment rights. After their victory in the trial court, defendant Miller was murdered and defendant Layton disappeared. Thus, when the U.S. government appealed the case to the U.S. Supreme Court, no written or oral argument on behalf of the defendants was presented to the Supreme Court.

Gun prohibitionists often cite this case for the proposition that the court held that the Second Amendment only protected the right of the states' National Guard to have government issued arms (i.e., the "Collective Rights" theory). This is an untruth. In fact, the court held that the entire populace constituted the "militia," and that the Second Amendment protected the right of the individual to keep and bear militia-type arms.

Recounting the long history of the "militia" in the colonies and the states, and the Constitutional Convention, the court stated that these "show plainly enough that the Militia comprised all males physically capable of acting in concert for the common defense."

The court also made clear that it was the private arms of these men that were protected. "[O]rdinarily when called for service these men were expected to appear bearing arms supplied by themselves and of the kind in common use at the time." Recounting the origins of this all inclusive "militia," the court quoted historian H.L. Osgood: "In all the colonies, as in England, the militia system was based on the principle of the assize of arms. This implied the general obligation of all adult male inhabitants to possess arms . . .". The court referred to various colonial militia statutes which required the individual ownership of arms and ammunition by its citizens. In setting forth this definition of the militia, the court implicitly rejected the "Collective Rights" view that the Second Amendment guarantees a right only to the organized military forces of the states.

Weapons Must Have a Militia-Type Purpose

The court held that the defendants' right to possess arms was limited to those arms that had a "militia" purpose. In that regard, it remanded the case to the trial court for an evidentiary hearing on whether or not a short barreled shotgun has some reasonable relationship to the preservation or efficiency of the militia. Thus, in order for a firearm to be constitutionally protected, the court held, the firearm should be a militia-type arm.

But the court did not require that Miller and Layton (neither of whom were members of the National Guard or Armed Forces) be members of the National Guard or Armed Forces in order to claim Second Amendment protection. Nor did the Supreme Court remand the case for the trial court to determine whether Miller and Layton were members of the National Guard or Armed Forces. Clearly, under the court's ruling, Miller and Layton had a right to claim individual Second Amendment protection, even if they were not members of the National Guard or Armed Forces. Thus, the case stands for the proposition that "the people," as individuals (not the states), had the constitutionally protected Second Amendment right to keep and bear any arms that could be appropriate for militia-type use.

Lewis v. United States involved a Fifth Amendment challenge to the federal law prohibiting the possession of firearms by convicted felons. The court noted that convicted felons are subject to the loss of numerous fundamental rights, including the right to vote, hold office, etc. The court thus found that this federal prohibition was not violative of the Fifth Amendment. In a footnote, the Court, citing *United States v. Miller*, reaffirmed that a firearm, in order to be constitutionally protected, must have a militia-type purpose. As in the *Miller* case, the court did not hold that a person must be a member of the Armed Forces in order to assert Second Amendment protections.

A number of recent United States Supreme Court cases have referred to the Second Amendment as a fundamental individual right. In *Moore v. City of East Cleveland*, a Fourteenth Amendment due process case, the Supreme Court put the right to keep and bear arms in company with other individual rights guaranteed by the Bill of Rights: "the freedom of speech, press, and religion; the right to keep and bear arms; the freedom from unreasonable searches and seizures . . .". In *Planned Parenthood of Southeastern Pa. v. Casey*, an abortion case, the Supreme Court again quoted Justice Harlan's above noted list of individual rights.

Individual Citizens Are "the People"

In *United States v. Verdugo-Urquirdez*, a Fourth Amendment case, the Supreme Court interpreted the meaning of the term "the people" in the Bill of Rights. The court stated that the term "the people" in the Second Amendment had the same meaning as in the Preamble to the Constitution and in the First, Fourth, and Ninth Amendments. In other words, the term "the people" means at least all citizens and legal aliens in the United States. This case thus makes clear that the Second Amendment is an individual right that applies to individual law-abiding Americans.

Contrary to the assertion of the gun prohibitionists, the Second Amendment protects the same "people" as the other rights guaranteed in the Bill of Rights; namely you and me. This, of course, is entirely in keeping with the intent of the drafters of the Bill of Rights and also the Supreme Court's interpretation of the individual rights guaranteed in the Bill of Rights.

"The Second Amendment poses no obstacle to reasonable gun control laws. No obstacle whatsoever."

The Second Amendment Does Not Protect Private Gun Ownership

Rachana Bhowmik

In the following viewpoint, Rachana Bhowmik argues that the Second Amendment's "right to bear arms" was not intended to protect individual gun ownership, but rather to safeguard the right of states to maintain organized militias. Bhowmik asserts that the idea gun control laws are unconstitutional is a "fraud" perpetrated by pro-gun organizations such as the National Rifle Association. The author concludes that Congress should stop pretending that gun ownership is constitutionally protected, and instead pass meaningful gun control legislation that will reduce gun violence. Bhowmik is a staff attorney with the Center to Prevent Handgun Violence's Legal Action Project, which helps represent victims of gun violence in suing gun manufacturers.

As you read, consider the following questions:

1. What did the Supreme Court conclude was the purpose of the Second Amendment in *United States v. Miller*, as quoted by the author?
2. What did the Framers of the Constitution mean by the term "militia," in the author's view?
3. What did the Framers mean by the phrase "bear arms," according to Bhowmik?

Reprinted from Rachana Bhowmik, "Our Second Amendment Rights Are Not Eroded," *Church and Society*, May/June 2000, by permission of the Presbyterian Church USA.

"[The Second Amendment] has been the subject of one of the greatest pieces of frauds, and I repeat the word "fraud" on the American public by special interest groups that I have ever seen in my lifetime."

—Former Chief Justice Warren Burger, appearing on the *MacNeil-Lehrer News Hour*, December16, 1991.

In the contentious debate over gun control, opponents of reasonable gun laws regularly argue that even the smallest form of regulation infringes upon Americans' "Second Amendment right" to own guns. This argument is without legal or historical support. In fact, the Second Amendment does not provide an individual with the right to bear arms. As the Supreme Court stated in *United States v. Miller,* more than 60 years ago, the Second Amendment was designed "to assure the continuation and render possible the effectiveness" of the state militia and the Amendment "must be interpreted and applied with that end in view." The federal courts have consistently echoed the view that the Second Amendment guarantees a right to be armed only to persons using the arms in service to an organized state militia. President Nixon's Solicitor General and former dean of Harvard Law School, Erwin Griswold, declared, "that the Second Amendment poses no barrier to strong gun laws is perhaps the most well-settled proposition in American Constitutional Law."

The Most Misunderstood Right

Despite this well-established proposition, one recent aberrant lower court decision, *U.S. v. Emerson*, has garnered significant media and public attention. In that decision, the district court went against *all federal court precedent* and found that a federal law prohibiting an individual under a domestic restraining order from possessing a firearm violates the individual's Second Amendment right. The individual in that case, a Timothy Joe Emerson, had threatened his estranged wife and child with a firearm and had threatened to kill his estranged wife's friends. He boasted to friends that he owned automatic weapons and needed only to purchase ammunition to prepare for a visit to his wife, in violation of a protective order. The district court decision overturning Timothy Joe Emerson's indictment is currently under appeal to the Fifth Circuit and most likely will be overturned.

Unfortunately, an unrelenting campaign of misinformation by the National Rifle Association (NRA) and others opposed to any regulations on firearms in this country has given much of the American public a warped understanding of the Second Amendment. While most Americans won't pretend to know what the Eighth Amendment provides, many Americans will quickly quote the Second as "the right to bear arms." That truncated reading, which you can also find on the NRA's national headquarters, overlooks the important first half of the Amendment. The amendment in full reads, "A well-regulated militia, being necessary to the security of a free state, the right of the people to keep and bear arms, shall not be infringed." Conveniently, over half of the amendment is omitted in the NRA's version, which focuses only on the words "the right to keep and bear arms." Because of the gun lobby, the Second Amendment may well be the most misunderstood of all the Bill of Rights.

A State's Right

Such a skewed focus ignores the history and the true intent of the Second Amendment. When the Second Amendment was drafted, most states were concerned with maintaining a viable state militia to defend the state against any possible invasion. A "militia" as the framers understood it, was "an organized, state-sponsored group of individuals acting in defense of the whole." Article I, section 8 of the Constitution granted Congress the power "[t]o provide for organizing, arming, and disciplining, the Militia, and for governing such Part of them as may be employed in the Service of the United States"—a grant of power that necessarily implies governmental organization of the group. In Federalist 29, Alexander Hamilton acknowledged that because a truly "well-regulated militia" would require frequent "military exercises and evolutions"—such a requirement would be a "serious public inconvenience and loss." Hamilton believed a more reasonable approach would be to ensure that militia members were "properly armed and equipped" and to "assemble them once or twice in the course of a year." James Madison, similarly, described a militia as a group of citizens "united and conducted by governments possessing their affections and confidence."

The use of the phrase "bear arms" further illustrates the military connotations of the Second Amendment. To "bear arms" means to possess weapons for military use. As historian Garry Wills has said "one does not bear arms against a rabbit." Indeed, the definition, then and now, of the word "arms" has a primarily military connotation. The term "arms" refers to instruments used in war. Accordingly, the Second Amendment was not meant to protect the rights of hunters and sportsmen, as some interpret it now, but was purely a means of protecting a state's right to maintain an armed force.

In addition to the Framers' understanding of the terms "militia" and "bear arms," we must understand why the Second Amendment was passed. It is important for modern day readers to recognize that the Constitution was drafted for a then untested national power. Out of concern for a possible abuse of powers by the federal government, the Framers drafted a Bill of Rights, which were designed to amend the Constitution "in order to prevent misconstruction or abuse of its powers." The debates among the states reflected a fear that giving Congress excessive power over the militia would enable Congress not only to regulate the militia, but also to disarm it completely, leaving the states defenseless against the federal government. In this sense, the state militias were thought to function as the "bulwarks of liberties." The state militias were properly preserved in the Bill of Rights as an important mechanism to enforce the limits on the federal government.

Never Intended as a Barrier to Gun Control

The Second Amendment was never intended to provide a constitutional right for individuals to own any and all firearms. In fact, as historian Michael Bellesiles has noted, when the Second Amendment was drafted, gun control laws were the norm in most of the colonies. Contrary to the image portrayed by the gun lobby, guns in those days were rare and expensive. As a result, colonial legislatures from New Hampshire to South Carolina imposed communal storage of firearms and permitted them to be removed only in times of crisis or for "muster day"—the day when the militia would perform its drills. The newly formed states implemented strict laws on gun possession—and historian Saul Cornell has recognized that in most states only the adult, white male population was allowed to own firearms, and even then they were subject to further restriction. In the mid-eighteenth century, Maryland forbade ownership of guns by Catholics and seized the weapons of any eligible male who refused to serve in the militia. In Pennsylvania, over half of the eligible gun-owning population, meaning free, white adult males, were deemed to lack the virtue necessary for the possession of firearms. Again, contrary to the public's understanding, the history is clear that our founding fathers lived during a time of strict gun control.

A *Well-Regulated* Militia

It's the simplest thing: a well-regulated militia. If the militia—which is what we now call the National Guard—essentially has to be well-regulated, in heaven's name why shouldn't we regulate 14-, 15-, and 16-year old kids having handguns or hoodlums having machine guns? I was raised on a farm, and we had guns around the house all the time. So I'm not against guns, but the National Rifle Association has done one of the most amazing jobs of misrepresenting and misleading the public.

Warren Burger, *USA Today*, December 16, 1991.

So why all the fuss? Why do the NRA and opponents of gun control bemoan the trampling of "Second Amendment rights" whenever a modest gun control law is proposed—be it background checks at gun shows or bans of cop-killing bullets and military-style assault weapons? Why is it that recent polls show 80 percent of Americans are in favor of stricter gun control laws, but over 60 percent think the Second Amendment must be repealed in order to achieve such goals?

Clearly, as former Chief Justice Warren Burger recognized, the American public has fallen prey to a "fraud." The campaign of misinformation regarding the Second Amendment is only intended to mislead Americans into believing that we are Constitutionally confined to the scourge of gun violence in this country. If Americans and politicians believe that gun ownership is a constitutional right—without qualification—they will be less likely to enact any restrictions on their use. The politicians who voted down a three day waiting period, who voted down mandatory child safety locks, who voted against the prohibition of the importation of high capacity ammunition clips, all hoped the American people would excuse their inaction as "constitutionally based." Often, the gun lobby relies on the Second Amendment because they have no rational argument for their opposition to reasonable measures such as background checks or safe storage laws. The American people should no longer give politicians such an easy out.

No Obstacle Whatsoever

The bottom line is that the Second Amendment poses no obstacle to reasonable gun control laws. No obstacle whatsoever. There is nothing unconstitutional about waiting periods—there is no constitutional right to access a gun whenever the urge strikes. There is no constitutional right to own a weapon without knowing proper safety procedures. There is no constitutional protection of a person's ability to purchase weapons without licensing and registration. Indeed, history shows that our forefathers knew who had weapons at all times. The licensing of gun owners is clearly in line with the "well-regulated" idea our forefathers had for their militias.

Meanwhile, despite the founding fathers' reliance on gun regulations, our country has adopted an almost cavalier attitude toward gun control laws. Most notable are the concealed carry laws that allow people to carry weapons most anywhere they please. In Texas in 1995, Governor George W. Bush signed into law a provision preventing churches and schools from prosecuting those who entered with weapons unless the state-provided signs were posted. As a result, when the Fort Worth, Texas, killer entered the church chapel on September 16 of 1999, if he possessed a concealed carry permit, the church would not have been able to prosecute him until he started shooting. Lax laws like these do not serve any "militia-purpose" and therefore are not protected by the Second Amendment. These lenient laws serve only to protect the criminally inclined.

As Americans we should not resign ourselves to the violence on our streets and in our schools. While high profile events like the Columbine massacre rock the nation, gun crimes have decreased nationwide. That means laws like the Brady Bill work to reduce gun violence in our country. But we can do more. As we approach the next millennium, the American people—gun owners and non-gun owners alike—must ensure that their elected leaders do all that is within their power to create laws that will prevent violence and see to it that such laws are enforced. Unfortunately, we have listened for too long to propaganda that any law regulating guns is an infringement of some inalienable right. We needn't listen any longer. Now is the time to listen to not only what the courts and history tell us, but what common sense tells us. We know we want to provide the children of this country with safe schools and safe streets. We know we don't want firearms in the hands of criminals and children. We know we want gun owners to be responsible in the care of their firearms. We know we want this vision of safe and healthy communities realized.

> *"Not only does the Congress not have the power to abolish that right [to self-defense], but Congress may not even infringe upon that right."*

The Second Amendment Protects the Inalienable Right to Self-Defense

Larry Craig

Larry Craig is a Republican senator from Idaho and a board member of the National Rifle Association. The following viewpoint is excerpted from Craig's June 6, 2000, remarks on the floor of the U.S. Senate during a debate on gun control legislation. Craig argues that such legislation must not infringe on citizens' right to defend themselves with a firearm. He claims that the Second Amendment protects an individual's right to self-defense, and he further asserts that, under the Constitution, Congress has no power to abolish or infringe upon that right. Craig lists examples of how guns are often used in self-defense, which he believes gun control advocates tend to ignore.

As you read, consider the following questions:
1. According to the author, what does President Clinton believe the Second Amendment should protect?
2. Why is the right to self-defense fundamental to freedom, in Craig's opinion?
3. What happens every 13 seconds in America, according to Craig?

Reprinted from Larry Craig's speech before the U.S. Senate, June 6, 2000.

Mr. President, I appear on the floor to speak about a provision of the Constitution of our country that has been under nearly constant attack for 8 years. In fact, we heard on the floor this morning two Senators speak about provisions in law that would alter a constitutional right.

The provision I am talking about is part of our Bill of Rights—the first 10 amendments to our Constitution—which protect our most basic rights from being stripped away by an overly zealous government, including rights that all Americans hold dear:

The freedom to worship according to one's conscience;

The freedom to speak or to write whatever we might think;

The freedom to criticize our Government;

And, the freedom to assemble peacefully.

Among the safeguards of these fundamental rights, we find the Second Amendment. Let me read it clearly:

A well regulated Militia, being necessary to the security of a free State, the right of the people to keep and bear Arms, shall not be infringed.

I want to repeat that.

The Second Amendment of our Constitution says very clearly that 'A well regulated Militia' is 'necessary' for the 'security of a free State,' and that 'the right of the people to keep and bear Arms, shall not be infringed.'

Gun Control Infringes on the Right to Self-Defense

What we heard this morning was an effort to infringe upon that right.

Some—even of my colleagues—will read what I have just quoted from our Constitution quite differently. They might read 'A well regulated Militia,' and stop there and declare that 'the right of the people to keep and bear Arms' actually means that it is a right of our Government to keep and bear arms because they associate the militia with the government. Yet, under this standard, the Bill of Rights would protect only the right of a government to speak, or the right of a government to criticize itself, if you were taking that same argument and transposing it over the First Amendment. In fact, the Bill of Rights protects the rights of people from being infringed upon by Government—not the other way around.

Of course, we know that our Founding Fathers in their effort to ratify the Constitution could not convince the citizens to accept it until the Bill of Rights was established to assure the citizenry that we were protecting the citizens from Government instead of government from the citizens.

Others say that the Second Amendment merely protects hunting and sport shooting. They see shooting competitions and hunting for food as the only legitimate uses of guns, and, therefore, conclude that the Second Amendment is no impediment to restricting gun use to those purposes.

You can hear it in the way President Clinton assures hunters that his gun control proposals will not trample on recreation—though his proposals certainly walk all over their rights.

In fact, the Second Amendment does not merely protect sport shooting and hunting, though it certainly does that.

Nor does the Second Amendment exist to protect the government's right to bear arms.

The framers of our Constitution wrote the Second Amendment with a greater purpose.

They made the Second Amendment the law of the land because it has something very particular to say about the rights of every man and every woman, and about the relationship of every man and every woman to his or her Government.

That is: The first right of every human being, the right of self-defense.

An Inalienable Right

Let me repeat that: The first right of every human being is the right of self-defense. Without that right, all other rights are meaningless. The right of self-defense is not something the government bestows upon its citizens. It is an inalienable right, older than the Constitution itself. It existed prior to government and prior to the social contract of our Constitution. It is the right that government did not create and therefore it is a right that under our Constitution the government simply cannot take away. The framers of our Constitution understood this clearly. Therefore, they did not merely acknowledge that the right exists. They denied Congress the power to infringe upon that right.

Under the social contract that is the Constitution of the United States, the American people have told Congress explicitly that we do not have the authority to abolish the American people's right to defend themselves. Further, the framers said not only does the Congress not have the power to abolish that right, but Congress may not even infringe upon that right. That is what our Constitution says. That is what the Second Amendment clearly lays out. Our Founding Fathers wrote the Second Amendment to tell us that a free state cannot exist if the people are denied the right or the means to defend themselves.

Let me repeat that because it is so fundamental to our freedom. A free state cannot exist, our free state of the United States collectively, cannot exist without the right of the people to defend themselves. This is the meaning of the Second Amendment. Over the years a lot of our citizens and many politicians have tried to nudge that definition around. But contrary to what the media and the President say, the right to keep and bear arms is as important today as it was 200 years ago.

Every day in this country thousands of peaceful, law-abiding Americans use guns to defend themselves, their families, and their property. Oftentimes, complete strangers are protected by that citizen who steps up and stops the thief or the stalker or the rapist or the murderer from going at that citizen.

The Importance of Firearms for Self-Defense

According to the FBI, criminals used guns in 1998 380,000 times across America. Yet research indicates that peaceful, law-abiding Americans, using their constitutional right, used a gun to prevent 2.5 million crimes in America that year and nearly every year. In fact, I believe the benefits of protecting the people's right to keep and bear arms far outweighs the destruction wrought by criminals and firearms accidents. The Centers for Disease Control report 32,000 Americans died from firearm injuries in 1997; under any estimate, that is a tragedy. Unfortunately, the Centers for Disease Control do not keep data on the number of lives that were saved when guns were used in a defensive manner.

Yet if we were to survey the public every year, we would find 400,000 Americans report they used a gun in a way that almost certainly saved either their life or someone else's. Is that estimate too high? Perhaps. I hope it is, because every time a life is saved from violence, that means that someone was threatening a life with violence. But that number would have to be over 13 times too high for our opponents to be correct when they say that guns are used to kill more often than they are used to protect. What they have been saying here and across America simply isn't true and the facts bear that out.

Reprinted by permission of Chuck Asay and Creators Syndicate. © 1999 Creators Syndicate, Inc.

We are not debating the tragedy. We are debating facts at this moment. They cannot come up with 2.5 million gun crimes. But clearly, through surveys, we can come up with 2.5 million crimes thwarted every year when someone used a gun in defense of themselves or their property. In many cases, armed citizens not only thwarted crime, but they held the suspect until the authorities arrived and placed that person in custody.

Stories of people defending themselves with guns do not make the nightly news. It just simply isn't news in America.

It isn't hot. It isn't exciting. It is American. Sometimes when people act in an American way, it simply isn't reportable in our country anymore. So the national news media doesn't follow it.

Yet two of the school shootings that have brought gun issues to the forefront, in Pearl, Mississippi, and Edinboro, Pennsylvania, were stopped by peaceful gun owners using their weapons to subdue the killer until the police arrived. How did that get missed in the story? It was mentioned once, in passing, and then ignored as people ran to the floor of the Senate to talk about the tragedy of the killing. Of course the killing was a tragedy, but it was also heroic that someone used their constitutional right to save lives in the process.

A third school shooting in Springfield, Oregon, was stopped because some parents took time to teach their child the wise use of guns. So when that young man heard a particular sound coming from the gun, he was able to rush the shooter, because he knew that gun had run out of ammunition. He was used to guns. He was around them. He subdued the shooter and saved potentially many other lives. We have recognized him nationally for that heroic act, that young high school student of Springfield, Oregon.

Pro-Gun Stories Ignored

For some reason, my colleagues on the other side of the aisle never want to tell these stories. They only want to say, after a crisis such as this, 'Pass a new gun control law and call 9-1-1.' Yet these stories are essential to our understanding of the right of people to keep and bear arms.

I will share a few of these stories right now. Shawnra Pence, a 29-year-old mother from Sequim, Washington, home alone with one of her children, heard an intruder break into the house. She took her .9 mm, took her child to the bedroom, and when the 18-year-old criminal broke into the bedroom, she said, 'Get out of my house, I have a gun, get out now.' He left and the police caught him. She saved her life and her child's life. It made one brief story in the *Peninsula Daily News* in Sequim, Washington.

We have to talk about these stories because it is time America heard the other side of this debate. There are 2.5

million Americans out there defending themselves and their property by the use of their constitutional right.

In Cumberland, Tennessee, a 28-year-old Jason McCulley broke into the home of Stanley Horn and his wife, tied up the couple at knife-point, and demanded to know where the couple kept some cash. While Mrs. Horn was directing the robber, Mr. Horn wriggled free from his restraints, retrieved his handgun, shot the intruder, and then called the police. The intruder, Jason McCulley, subsequently died. If some Senators on the other side of the aisle had their way, perhaps the Horns would have been killed and Jason McCulley would have walked away.

Earlier today, we heard the Senator from Illinois and the Senator from California read the names of people killed by guns in America. Some day they may read the name Jason McCulley. I doubt they will tell you how he died, however, because it doesn't advance their goal of destroying the Second Amendment. But as Paul Harvey might say: Now you know the rest of the story.

Every 13 seconds this story is repeated across America. Every 13 seconds in America someone uses a gun to stop a crime. Why do our opponents never tell these stories? Why do the enemies of the right to keep and bear arms ignore this reality that is relived by 2.5 million Americans every year? Why is it that all we hear from them is, 'Pass a new gun control law, and, by the way, call 9-1-1.'. . .

Safeguarding the Second Amendment

Having said all of this, let there be no mistake. Guns are not for everyone. We restrict children's access to guns and we restrict criminals' access to guns, but we must not tolerate politicians who tell us that the Second Amendment only protects the right to hunt. We must not tolerate politicians who infringe upon our right to defend ourselves from thieves and stalkers and rapists and murderers. And we must not tolerate the politician who simply says: 'Pass another gun control law and call 9-1-1.'

"An individual's right to own and bear arms, as well as actually to use them, must be balanced by the greater social needs of a society and its citizens' right to safety."

The Second Amendment Is Not Absolute

Michael W. Warfel

In the following viewpoint, Michael W. Warfel argues that while the Bill of Rights does protect an individual's right to own firearms, the right to bear arms is not absolute. He describes a high-caliber rifle that is capable of shooting down aircraft, as well as weapons such as howitzers or missile launchers, as examples of firearms that individuals should not have the right to own. He also rebuts the National Rifle Association's claim that any restrictions on firearm ownership will inevitably lead to a total ban. Finally, Warfel concedes that new gun control legislation will not solve the problem of gun violence in America—but he insists that is a vital first step. Warfel, a Catholic priest, is the bishop of the Diocese of Juneau, Alaska.

As you read, consider the following questions:

1. According to the *New York Times* article Warfel cites, what are the requirements for buying the .50-caliber 82A1 rifle, as compared to the requirements for buying a handgun?
2. According to the author, what aspect of modern society could the framers of the Bill of Rights not have envisioned?
3. What analogies does Warfel make between owning a car and owning a gun?

A number of years ago, when I was a parish priest, a woman preparing for baptism at Easter asked if she could speak with me privately. There were various issues that had been bothering her, and she wished to discuss them. I had come to know her somewhat during the preceding months and appreciated the sincerity with which she viewed her formation as a Catholic. Baptism for her was not a light matter.

Shortly after we began to converse, the issue of gun control surfaced. This woman, in her mid-30's, was a member of the National Rifle Association and had some very definite views about any type of gun control legislation. Her views were strong for a number of reasons. She enjoyed spending time with her husband shooting targets at the local shooting range. She valued the relationships she had formed with other members of her shooting club, many of whom were upstanding members of the community. She looked forward to the annual fall moose and deer hunting seasons not only as a time to commune with nature—as well as to have additional time with family and friends—but also as an important opportunity to put meat in the freezer. For many Alaskan families, subsistence hunting is an indispensable source of food and a way to supplement the family income.

The Second Amendment Is Not Sacred

I listened for some time to her concerns. Guns obviously were a part of her lifestyle, and she had recently become apprehensive after hearing some parish members express the need for gun control. The whole time that she spoke, she kept referring to the Second Amendment to the Bill of Rights, which affirms the right of citizens to own and bear arms. As she continued to speak (now becoming more animated and beginning to monopolize the conversation), a certain realization came to me. She was speaking of the Second Amendment as if it were the second commandment of the Decalogue from the Bible. She had elevated the Bill of Rights to the level of a holiness code. For her, the right to own and bear arms, and to do so with minimal limitations, were God-given rights and therefore sacred.

This woman, a person seeking to embrace a life in Christ,

was deeply concerned that if gun control legislation were enacted, she would have to surrender a significant part of her lifestyle—a part that she had considered to be not only not sinful, but wholesome. In addition, she saw her right to possess guns as virtually a sacred one. How could members of the church she planned to join possibly be against something that was sacred? What she failed to perceive was the relative nature of the Second Amendment. While I believe that the way she used firearms was not inconsistent with her new-found faith, this cannot be said of all gun use.

The Right to Own Firearms Is Not Absolute

The right to private property (in this case guns) is not absolute. An individual's right to own and bear arms, as well as actually to use them, must be balanced by the greater social needs of a society and its citizens' right to safety. There are good reasons why restrictions may need to be placed on the possession and use of firearms. With regard to certain types and classes of firearms, even the possibility of possessing them is bad for society.

I cite an example that recently has been in the news, the Barrett .50-caliber 82A1 rifle. It is a military weapon designed to destroy armor-reinforced vehicles or even shoot down low-flying aircraft. It has an effective range of about one mile. Ammunition for it is available on the civilian market. Though somewhat pricey (about $6,000), it is a relatively easy purchase. According to a recent *New York Times* article, "Gun dealers may sell anyone a .50-caliber if buyers present identification showing they are 18 years old and have no felony convictions." By contrast, to buy a handgun, individuals must prove that they are at least 21. A .50-caliber rifle hardly seems to be a sporting rifle!

A majority of Americans admit that there is need for some kind of gun control. A recent Harris Poll demonstrated that 69 percent of all Americans and 57 percent of America's gun owners want tougher gun control laws. Likewise, a recent CNN/*Time* magazine poll found that six out of ten Americans generally favored stricter gun control laws. Of those interviewed, 76 percent favored federal laws requiring the registration of all handguns, and 77 percent favored the licensing of all handgun owners. Americans do not support a total ban, but they do support restrictions. For most, it is a matter of agreeing on where the line ought to be drawn. Few people would argue that the Second Amendment gives an individual the right to possess and use a 175 millimeter howitzer or a hand-held missile launcher. There are some, though, who would argue that they have the right to possess a Barrett .50-caliber rifle.

Firearms Should Be Regulated, Registered, and Licensed

The framers of the Bill of Rights envisioned the Second Amendment during a time when the United States was a fledgling nation. In all probability, they could not have imagined the levels of violence that confront Americans in today's society. We live amid what has been termed a "culture of violence." While there is some evidence that violent crime may have lessened recently, Americans still murder each other with guns 19 times more often than do the people of the 25 other wealthiest nations. In addition, among the 36 wealthiest, the United States has the highest proportion of suicides from guns. While it is claimed that guns may be necessary to protect oneself and one's loved ones, they may just as likely be used to provide criminals or mentally ill people with easy access to the means to cause irrevocable harm.

I believe that the government has a responsibility to its citizens to limit access to certain types of firearms, as well as to set the parameters under which its citizens may exercise their Second Amendment rights. An analogous example commonly cited is that of the restrictions placed on owning and operating a motor vehicle. Cars are registered and licensed, just as are their operators. "Rules of the road" stipulate how a driver may use his or her vehicle. These rules place limitations on drivers, not as a punishment, but as a way to ensure the welfare and safety of travelers. While the "rules of the road" may vary from state to state, they are largely consistent in order to make the roads of the nation safe. Obviously, these rules are sometimes broken, and people are injured and killed. And sometimes they may seem not to apply, such as the rule that requires a stop at a red light at 2 a.m. when no other car is in sight. Yet we would be far worse off without them. Sensible regulation of firearms is just as reasonable.

A Sensitive Issue

Gun control is a sensitive matter for many Americans on both sides of the issue. In all probability, it will be an issue during [the 2000] presidential election. There is the perception by some gun owners that those who want greater gun control would like to eliminate guns altogether. An article on the National Rifle Association's official Web site is entitled, "Gun Control = Gun Prohibition." Any restrictions on gun ownership are viewed as a slippery slope toward total elimination. As someone once said, "That's not very likely to happen until the lion lies down with the lamb. And it won't be the result of any legislative action." Fear that restrictions on firearms will lead to their complete elimination, however, seems based more on paranoia than reason.

The American Civil Liberties Union on Gun Control

If indeed the Second Amendment provides an absolute, constitutional protection for the right to bear arms in order to preserve the power of the people to resist government tyranny, then it must allow individuals to possess bazookas, torpedoes, SCUD missiles and even nuclear warheads, for they, like handguns, rifles and M-16s, are arms. Moreover, it is hard to imagine any serious resistance to the military without such arms. Yet few, if any, would argue that the Second Amendment gives individuals the unlimited right to own any weapons they please. But as soon as we allow governmental regulation of any weapons, we have broken the dam of Constitutional protection. Once that dam is broken, we are not talking about whether the government can constitutionally restrict arms, but rather what constitutes a reasonable restriction.

American Civil Liberties Union, "Gun Control," 1996, www.aclu.org/library/aaguns.html.

I believe a majority of Americans recognize that there are legitimate uses for guns: competitive shooting and recreation, use by police officers and military personnel and hunting. I myself have carried a .44-caliber magnum pistol for protection when hiking in bear country in Alaska, and I would hope to be able to continue the practice. I have acquaintances who prevented an almost certain mauling (and probably death) because they were able to protect themselves against a charging bear with a firearm. In the present culture of violence, however, a broader perspective than back-country Alaska must be included. It is only reasonable to place appropriate and sensible restrictions on the possession and use of firearms for the well-being of the nation as a whole.

While some areas of the United States seem to be more prone to violence than others, no area is particularly safe or unscathed. Even in Alaska, there have been school shootings. For reasonable controls to be effective, regulations must be made on a federal level, like the Brady Bill. Without national legislation, it is simply too easy to transfer firearms across state boundaries.

Stricter Gun Controls Cannot Provide a Complete Solution

Will restrictions on the possession and use of firearms totally solve the problem of gun violence? Hardly. Violence in society is recognizably a complex problem fed by a number of forces. The U.S. Catholic bishops' statement *Confronting a Culture of Violence* (1994) lists a number of influences beyond firearms, such as the disintegration of family life, violence in media, substance abuse, gangs and youth violence and poverty.

One particularly important factor that appears to be eroding America's sensitivity to violence in general is the manner in which violence is used in the media. Lt. Col. Dave Grossman, author of *On Killing: The Psychological Cost of Learning to Kill in War and Society*, describes how a combination of desensitization (brutalization), classical conditioning, operant conditioning and role modeling by the use of violence in media have "trained" countless people in our society to accept violence. He notes that it is the "newest variable" in developed nations that are experiencing record levels of violent crime. We view bloodshed and gore on television and movies and play violent video games while eating popcorn.

Violence becomes a game and something for entertainment.

Simply establishing stricter gun control laws is hardly the total solution to gun violence. Any long-term solution must address a multitude of factors in addition to violence in the media: poverty, the breakup of family, abuse, drug use. Still, while restrictions on firearms may not offer the total solution to gun violence, they are definitely an important piece of the puzzle. Also, any solution ought to include the enforcement of existing gun laws and the prosecution of criminals engaged in violent acts.

It is true that society needs to address the many deep-seated problems that lead people to behave in violent ways. At the same time, given the present climate in which some people seem to turn so easily toward violent behavior, society needs to take steps to prevent instruments that can easily kill from too readily getting into the wrong hands, and insist that those who do possess them learn how to use them responsibly and safely.

"There is no such thing as a free nation where police and the military are allowed the force of arms but individual citizens are not."

The Second Amendment Safeguards Individual Liberty

Charlton Heston

Charlton Heston, an award-winning actor, is president of the National Rifle Association. He maintains in the following viewpoint that the right to private gun ownership is guaranteed by the Second Amendment, and moreover, that the right of private citizens to defend themselves with firearms is vital to freedom. Without the ability to defend themselves, Heston argues, individuals quickly fall prey to tyranny, either from the government or from other groups who are able to intimidate unarmed citizens. The right to bear arms, he concludes, was enshrined in the Constitution because it is vital to individual liberty.

As you read, consider the following questions:
1. How did all the genocides of the twentieth century begin, in Heston's view?
2. What do gun bans inevitably lead to, according to the author?
3. What quote by American statesman George Mason does Heston cite?

Reprinted from Charlton Heston, "The Second Amendment: America's First Freedom," *Human Rights*, Fall 1999. © 1999 by American Bar Association.

As Americans, we have rights no one can take away—because no one gave them to us. They were ours from birth. We each have a birth certificate, but it didn't give us life. It just put on paper what we already know: that we are alive.

Likewise, the Constitution doesn't give us rights. It just puts on paper what we already know: that we are free to say and write and think and work and worship as we choose. And we are free to own a firearm.

The Bill of Rights is simply a set of freedoms the framers specifically set aside as off limits to government meddling; rights that *we the people* reserve to ourselves as individuals, unequivocally and absolutely. They don't recognize color, class, creed, or wealth. And they don't just protect leaders or lawyers—but all of us, equally.

The beauty of the Constitution is the way it accounts for human nature. We aren't always a docile, benevolent, egalitarian species. We can be egotistical, vengeful, power mad, and sometimes even murderous. The Bill of Rights recognizes this and raises the ramparts needed to protect the individual.

America's First Freedom

In that regard, the Second Amendment is, in order of importance, *first*. Among our many freedoms—freedom of speech, of the press, of religion, of assembly, and the right to a redress of grievances—the Second Amendment is first among equals. There is no such thing as a free nation where police and the military are allowed the force of arms but individual citizens are not. Every genocide we've seen this century began with the denial of the right to bear arms. That doesn't mean gun bans lead to genocide. They just make genocide easier—and tyranny an inevitability. Tyranny doesn't necessarily have to come from government; it can come through the bedroom window or hang like a sullen shadow over the lives of those forced to live in fear.

Aristotle knew it 2,300 years ago, when he considered popular arms ownership the single most reliable indicator of whether a society was genuinely free. So did the Roman orator Cicero, who wrote, "There exists a law, not written down anywhere but inborn in our hearts; a law that comes to use from nature itself . . . that, if our lives are endangered, any and every method of protecting ourselves is morally right."

John Adams wrote, "Arms in the hands of citizens [may] be used at individual discretion . . . in private self defense." George Mason wrote, "To disarm the people is the best and most effectual way to enslave them." Thomas Jefferson wrote, "No man shall ever be debarred the use of arms." From the beginning, the essence and intent of the Second Amendment was that it be a right of individual citizens—a view that even long-time gun control advocate and constitutional scholar Laurence Tribe now endorses.

Cultural War on a Constitutional Right

Look at the world [that kids today] grow up in. They've never known the Great Depression, World War II, the Cold War, or the threat of nuclear annihilation. If they were even born by the time of Vietnam, it's at most a grainy memory. They've never known a world where the English begged for American firearms to defend themselves from an expected Nazi invasion. They've never known a world where high-school rifle teams were as common and as accepted as baseball teams or debating clubs. They've never known a world where the Second Amendment was anything but attacked, ignored, or assigned the blame for crimes of all kinds.

Schools teach against it. Churches preach against it. Teachers who don't understand or don't believe in the right to keep and bear arms pass on their ignorance and indifference. Textbooks claim the Second Amendment guarantees government's right to assemble a National Guard, or that it's a "collective right" of society or the states. The right to bear arms is misinterpreted, kids are told—or it doesn't exist at all. . . .

To those of us who have been around for a while, this is so absurd as to be laughable. But to young people today, it's all they hear and all they have ever known.

And soon, if not already, those young, impressionable minds will account for a decisive voting bloc in every national election. That's why I so strongly believe we must teach the next generation of Americans about the right to keep and bear arms.

Because if this society-wide cultural war against the Second Amendment continues, and young people aren't primed to understand its awesome importance, then firearm freedom could be forsaken and forgotten in just one generation.

Charlton Heston, *Saturday Evening Post*, January/February 2000.

A Natural Right

The Second Amendment guarantees us the absolute ability to defend ourselves from anyone who would take away our liberties or our lives, whether it be King George's Redcoats or today's criminal predators. It alone offers the capacity to live without fear. It is the one natural right that allows "rights" to exist at all.

History proves it. Common sense dictates it. And in the headlines and nightly news, that fundamental human freedom continually re-asserts itself as self-evident—from its denial to ethnic Albanians in Serbia, to its everyday exercise by citizens here at home, where the right to bear arms stops criminal attacks 2.5 million times every year.

*"Here's how to fix a flawed amendment that
is the source of so much confusion: Repeal
its ambiguous preamble."*

The Second Amendment Should Be Repealed

William Safire

In the following viewpoint, William Safire addresses the ambiguity of the wording of the Second Amendment: Americans are torn, he writes, over whether the amendment protects an individual's right to gun ownership or only the right of states to form militias. He proposes a solution. It is possible to nullify or amend one amendment with another amendment. Thus Congress could propose an amendment that unequivocally gives Americans the right to gun ownership. It would need to be ratified by the states, and in the process Americans could decide, through their votes, whether Americans should have the right to bear arms or not. Safire is a columnist for the *New York Times*.

As you read, consider the following questions:
1. What two views of the Second Amendment does Laurence H. Tribe call a "false statement of choice," as quoted by Safire?
2. Why, in Safire's words, shouldn't the Second Amendment be interpreted as a state's right sometimes and as an individual right at other times?
3. What, according to the author, is the "intellectually lazy" approach to the issue of gun control?

Reprinted, with permission, from William Safire, "An Appeal for Reason," *The New York Times*, June 10, 1999. Copyright © 1999 by The New York Times Co.

Amendment II: A well-regulated militia being necessary to the security of a free State, the right of the people to keep and bear Arms shall not be infringed.

Twenty years ago [in 1979], I asked Richard Nixon what he thought of gun control. His on-the-record reply: "Guns are an abomination." Free from fear of gun owners' retaliation at the polls, he favored making handguns illegal and requiring licenses for hunting rifles.

When ABC's Charles Gibson asked Bill Clinton why he was supporting only niminy-piminy restrictions on guns, our current President, also with the freedom of a lame duck, replied testily: "Should people have to register guns like they register their cars? Do I think that? Of course I do." He didn't propose it only because Congress was opposed.

What Does the Second Amendment Actually Mean?

The majority of the nation may well share the revulsion at firearms expressed by these two quite different Presidents. That is why Congress, using the loophole of protecting minors, is nibbling nervously at the fringes of gun control. We'll get trigger locks and a delay of sales at gun shows; big deal.

Why not bite the bullet? Wouldn't it be better to frame the argument in plain, stark terms?

Believers in unrestricted purchase and ownership of guns claim a personal right guaranteed under the Bill of Rights' Amendment II. They say the people's right "to keep and bear Arms" means exactly what it says.

Believers in gun control insist that the Founders wanted to insure that the states forming the Federal compact had the right to have militias, which each state would regulate; thus could Virginia put down a slave rebellion. They argue that the Second Amendment did not confer any right of an individual to carry a weapon.

Who's right? Or, whose right—is it the state's or the individual's? Until recently, advocates of gun control have argued successfully that the right belongs to the state, not the private person.

But that has recently been successfully challenged. A Federal court in Texas held that individuals have at least some rights to weapons. The appeals will probably put the argument before the Supreme Court.

This is not a lay-down hand for the anti-gun lobby. For years, principled liberals have had qualms about the way the Second Amendment has been treated as a quaint archaism to be ignored.

The Murky Second

Professor Laurence H. Tribe, Harvard's guru of constitutional law who supports gun control and would surely be on the high court if liberals had their way, told the [New York] Times: "It becomes impossible to deny that some right to bear arms is among the rights of American citizens."

A Relic of the Past

Why must we subordinate ourselves to a 208-year-old law that, if the latest scholarship is correct, is contrary to what the democratic majority believes is in its best interest? . . .

There is simply no solution to the gun problem within the confines of the U.S. Constitution. . . . Other countries are free to change their constitutions when it becomes necessary. In fact, with the exception of Luxembourg, Norway, and Great Britain, there is not one advanced industrial nation that has not thoroughly revamped its constitution since 1900. If they can do it, why can't we? Why must Americans remain slaves to the past?

Daniel Lazare, *Harper's*, October 1999.

Asked to elucidate, Professor Tribe tells me: "The debate has been cast in a misleading, dichotomous way between those who cast the Second Amendment as completely irrelevant to any claim of individual right and those who treat it as . . . essentially stripping the Government of the power to impose reasonable limits to protect public safety. That's a false statement of choice."

Comes now the emergence of a constitutional middle ground. The Murky Second is thus interpreted as a state right sometimes and as an individual right at other times. One day it's James Madison, the next day it's Madison James.

That can't be right. Put another way, a right that sometimes isn't is no right at all. After a great job on the First Amendment, the amending Founders botched the Second.

Let's Take a Vote on the Second Amendment

The intellectually lazy will say, "Let the Supremes [the Supreme Court] sort it out." I say, let the people decide a political issue. Either we're serious about our right to gun ownership or we're serious about our need for gun control.

Here's how to fix a flawed amendment that is the source of so much confusion: Repeal its ambiguous preamble. Let some member of Congress introduce an amendment to strike the words before the comma in the Second Amendment.

Then vote the amendment up or down. If it fails to pass, stop arguing and compromise on nibbling. If Congress passes repeal, let ratification be fought out in the states, where representatives closest to the people can decide on strict licensing.

That's the decisive, constitutional way to come to grips with the abomination of too many handguns in trigger-happy hands.

Periodical Bibliography

The following articles have been selected to supplement the diverse views presented in this chapter. Addresses are provided for periodicals not indexed in the *Readers' Guide to Periodical Literature*, the *Alternative Press Index*, the *Social Sciences Index*, or the *Index to Legal Periodicals and Books*.

Akhil Reed Amar	"Second Thoughts: What the Right to Bear Arms Really Means," *New Republic*, July 12, 1999.
Angie Cannon	"Rights and Wrongs on Guns: Importance of Obscure Texas Case, Wending Its Way Through Federal Courts, to Second Amendment," *U.S. News & World Report*, June 7, 1999.
Brian Doherty	"Tragic Government," *Reason*, May 1997.
Charlton Heston	"Our First Freedom," *Saturday Evening Post*, January/February 2000.
Wendy Kaminer	"Second Thoughts on the Second Amendment," *Atlantic Monthly*, March 1996.
Daniel Lazare	"Your Constitution Is Killing You," *Harper's*, October 1999.
Bob Levin	"Casualties of the Right to Bear Arms," *Maclean's*, May 3, 1999.
Nelson Lund	"Taking the Second Amendment Seriously," *Weekly Standard*, July 24, 2000.
Jon Meacham et al.	"'I Think the Real Target Is the Second Amendment': Interview with Wayne LaPierre," *Newsweek*, August 23, 1999.
Daniel D. Polsby	"Second Reading: Treating the Second Amendment as Normal Constitutional Law," *Reason*, March 1996.
Laurence H. Tribe	"Well-Regulated Militias, and More," *New York Times*, October 28, 1999.

CHAPTER 4

How Can Gun Violence Be Reduced?

Chapter Preface

Traditionally, debates over how to reduce gun violence have focused on the gun control controversy: Anti-gun groups have pushed for restrictions or bans on guns, while pro-gun groups have argued that criminals who use guns, not guns themselves, should be locked up. More recently, efforts to reduce gun violence have focused on new technologies that could make guns safer. One proposed approach to making guns safer is to install trigger locks, which would require the user to know the proper combination to fire the gun. A more advanced, so-called "smart gun" technology would recognize a user's thumbprint, so that only the owner of a gun could fire it.

Proponents of trigger locks and smart guns say that they are the equivalent of putting safety caps on bottles of poison. Gun makers have also supported the new technologies. "The industry definitely recognizes the appeal of a smart-gun technology," says Ken Jorgensen, a Smith & Wesson executive. "We realized there is a market of people who want a firearm that only they can put into operation."

But many gun owners are wary of the proposed technologies, which as of 2000 are still in the developmental stage. Researcher Gary Kleck cautions against government initiatives that would force gun makers to rush the new technologies: "Careful development and testing take time. An unreliable technology introduced too soon could hamper self-defense or lull owners into storing guns carelessly. And if the technology is too expensive, law-abiding low-income people, who are the most frequent crime victims, will be discouraged from acquiring guns for self-protection." Even gun control groups are wary of the hype surrounding "smart" guns. Kristen Rand, director of federal policy at the Violence Policy Center, says her organization opposes them because "we think ultimately their effect would be to sell more guns."

While trigger locks and smart guns could eventually help to make guns safer, clearly they are not a panacea. The authors in the following chapter suggest other measures that might reduce gun violence.

"Federal prosecutions of gun crimes have dropped by 44% during the Clinton-Gore Administration."

Stronger Enforcement of Existing Gun Control Laws Is Needed

Charlton Heston

The following viewpoint is excerpted from testimony that Charlton Heston, the president of the National Rifle Association, gave before the U.S. House of Representatives on November 4, 1999. In it, he rejects the idea that new, stronger gun control laws are needed to reduce gun violence. He points to Project Exile, a Virginia program in which local law enforcement, state prosecutors, and the Bureau of Alcohol, Tobacco, and Firearms (BATF) work together to aggressively prosecute criminals found in possession of a firearm. Heston says that in contrast to Virginia's program, the federal government has been lax in prosecuting gun crimes. The federal government should not pass new gun control legislation, he concludes, because it has failed to aggressively enforce the laws that are already on the books.

As you read, consider the following questions:

1. Of the 2,400 violent crimes committed with a firearm in Washington, D.C., in 1998, how many were prosecuted at the federal level, according to Heston?
2. How did a BATF official try to explain the drop in federal prosecutions of gun crimes, as quoted by the author?

Reprinted from remarks by Charlton Heston before the U.S. House Committee on Government Reform, Subcommittee on Criminal Justice, Drug Policy, and Human Resources, November 4, 1999.

J ust 150 miles from here, in sleepy Richmond, Virginia, they cut gun homicides by one-half in just one year. They employed the awesome simplicity of enforcing existing federal gun law. It's called Project Exile. The word is out on the streets of Richmond that, if you're a felon caught with a gun, you will go to jail for 5 years. They're actually changing criminal behavior and saving lives. That's not partisan, that's not conjecture, that's not hyperbole.

Thanks to those fearless prosecutors, innocent Americans are alive today in Richmond that would have died at the hands of armed felons.

Little Enforcement of Federal Gun Laws

But elsewhere across this land, innocent Americans alive today will be dead tomorrow or next month or next year . . . because this Administration, as a policy, is putting gun-toting felons on the streets in record numbers.

If you don't believe the NRA, believe the recent independent Syracuse University study that revealed federal prosecutions of gun crimes have dropped by 44% during the Clinton-Gore Administration.

Right here in our nation's capital, there were some 2,400 violent crimes committed with firearms in 1997. Guess how many of those armed criminals were prosecuted from federal referrals? Only two.

In fact, little old Richmond had more prosecutions under federal gun laws in 1998 than California, New Jersey, New York and Washington, D.C.—*combined*!

Why does the President ask for more federal gun laws if he's not going to enforce the ones we have? Why does the President ask for more police if he's not going to prosecute their arrests?

This deadly charade is killing people and surely will kill more. When political hot air is turning into cold blood . . . when duplicitous spin is becoming lethal . . . somebody's got to speak up.

No lives will be saved talking about how many hours a waiting period should be, or how many rounds a magazine should hold, or how cheap a Saturday Night Special should be.

But if you want to impact gun crime now, you will demand that Project Exile be implemented in major U.S. cities now.

The Success of Richmond's Project Exile

Project Exile is the product of a desire to explore creative alternative strategies to address the difficult urban problem of guns, drugs, and violent crime. The program was developed in 1996 from a successful partnership between the Richmond Police Department and the United States Attorney for the Eastern District of Virginia. . . .

From Project Exile's inception, the Bureau of Alcohol, Tobacco and Firearms (BATF) was brought on board as the sponsoring federal agency to become the third member of this new team. Agents from the local office are assigned, as part of the Project Exile Task Force, to aid our officers in their investigations and to "adopt" cases that meet certain criteria for prosecution within the federal courts system under 18 United States Code 922 and 924. Such criteria include gun possession while possessing drugs; gun possession by a convicted felon; gun possession if a person is a fugitive from another state; gun possession if under a felony indictment; gun possession if a person is the subject of a restraining order; gun possession by a drug user; gun possession if a person has been involved in prior domestic violence; or gun possession if the gun is known (by the possessor) to be stolen.

A "typical" Project Exile case would involve an officer, who might be assigned to a precinct beat car or to any other uniformed or plain clothes unit of our agency, encountering or arresting an individual who has used, or is in possession of, a firearm. If, during the course of the investigation of that incident, it is learned that the person meets any of the previously listed criteria, the case is referred to the Project Exile Task Force for review and possible adoption. . . .

The first Project Exile indictment was prosecuted in early 1997. As of October 1, 1999, in just two years, there have been 544 people indicted under Project Exile guidelines, which also has resulted in the removal of 650 guns from our city's streets. . . . Fewer drug dealers and users are being found carrying firearms. Thus, we are realizing a reduction in the previously high "carry rate." . . . Consequently, gun violence has been reduced.

Teresa P. Gooch, testimony before the U.S. House of Representatives, November 4, 1999.

I wish you luck. For a year we have challenged, urged and pleaded with the Clinton Administration to take 50 million dollars—out of a 14 billion dollar budget—and implement Project Exile's tough enforcement program nationwide.

Their response?

A Justice Department spokesman told *USA Today*, quote, ". . . it's not the federal government's role to prosecute" these gun cases.

Deputy Attorney General Eric Holder ridiculed Project Exile as a "cookie cutter" approach to fighting crime and called it "fundamentally wrong" to earmark funds for enforcing federal gun laws. Fundamentally wrong!

A senior official of the BATF tried to explain away the 44% decrease in federal prosecutions of gun crimes by saying, ". . . we seek to prosecute the few sharks at the top rather than the numerous guppies of the criminal enterprise."

Mr. Chairman, those "guppies" with guns are murdering innocent Americans who are left defenseless by a White House and a Justice Department that lack either the time or the spine to enforce existing laws against violent felons with guns.

We challenge Bill Clinton to direct Attorney General Janet Reno to call upon all of the district attorneys around the country, instructing them to take on just 10 more federal gun cases each month. That is their job. The result would be the prosecution of about 10,000 more violent felons with guns—10,000 potential murderers taken off the streets of America.

And we urge this body to do what the White House won't . . . to appropriate 50 million dollars to implement Project Exile in major cities across the country.

And if the President calls that "fundamentally wrong," ask him what you call it when the odds of doing time for armed crime are no worse than the flip of a coin.

> *"The enforcement of current [gun control] laws requires new laws—laws the NRA steadfastly opposes."*

Stronger Gun Control Laws Are Needed

New Republic

The *New Republic* is a weekly magazine of American politics, foreign policy, and culture. In the following viewpoint, the editors of the *New Republic* dispute the National Rifle Association's claim that federal gun control laws are not being adequately enforced. Federal prosecutions of gun crimes have increased, not decreased, since 1993, they claim. Moreover, argues the *New Republic*, truly aggressive prosecution of gun crimes requires new gun control laws. For example, loopholes in current legislation allow unlicensed gun dealers to easily accumulate a large stock of firearms, then sell them, often in an almost untraceable manner, to criminals. The NRA's call for the government to enforce existing law is hypocritical, conclude the *New Republic* editors, because the NRA has in the past vigorously opposed such efforts.

As you read, consider the following questions:
1. Who is responsible for prosecuting criminals who fail background checks, according to the authors?
2. What is the federal agency charged with enforcing gun laws, and how has NRA vice president Wayne LaPierre referred to its agents, as quoted by the *New Republic*?
3. What does the NRA really want, in the authors' view?

From "Yelling 'Fire!'" editorial, *The New Republic*, April 3, 2000. Reprinted by permission of *The New Republic*, © 2000, The New Republic, Inc.

O nce upon a time, the National Rifle Association made a principled argument: The Second Amendment guarantees people the right to bear arms, and the government shouldn't interfere. Yes, some people will die because guns are legal, but so what? Some people die because the Fourth Amendment keeps the government from busting into the houses of potential criminals. That's the cost of freedom.

The NRA's False Claims

We disagreed with that argument, but we respected it. But who can respect the NRA's transparent efforts to cast itself as the champion of existing gun-control laws? According to NRA Executive Vice President Wayne LaPierre, the Clinton administration hasn't prosecuted enough of the people who fail criminal background checks, as the Brady Bill requires. So felons stay on the street and commit more crimes. LaPierre's poster boy is Benjamin Smith, who last summer went on a shooting spree that left nine people wounded and two dead. As LaPierre tells it, Smith should have been arrested before his deadly rampage—when he tried to buy a gun from a licensed firearms dealer in Illinois and a background check turned up a restraining order. But Smith wasn't arrested; instead, he went to an unlicensed dealer, bought two handguns, and proceeded on his bloody mission. Enforcement of existing laws, LaPierre insists, not the establishment of new ones, would have prevented those murders.

But LaPierre's argument has almost no basis in reality. First, prosecutions for gun violations—at both the federal and state levels—have increased since Clinton took office. Second, in most states, including Illinois, the state authorities, not the feds, conduct background checks.

New Laws Are Needed

And these are only LaPierre's factual errors. His logic is worse. Simply put, the enforcement of current laws requires new laws—laws the NRA steadfastly opposes. The Smith case nicely illustrates the problem. Consider the unlicensed dealer who sold Smith his handguns. The dealer amassed his stock of guns by outmaneuvering a federal law that requires gun stores to report the sale of two or more guns at a time to the Bureau of Alcohol, Tobacco, and Firearms (ATF). He got around it by purchasing 65 handguns, one at a time, from the same store. This loophole could be easily closed with a new law that permitted only one handgun purchase a month, thereby preventing unlicensed dealers from amassing vast arsenals. But the NRA opposes this law. NRA lobbying has also kept private dealers in most states free to sell guns without conducting background checks and without keeping records of their sales. And, without those records, it is much harder to detect gun trafficking or enforce the current laws.

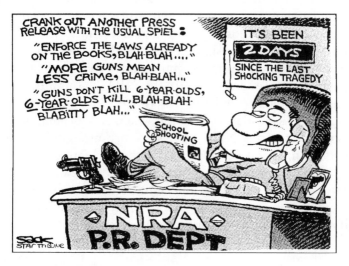

Steve Sack. © Tribune Media Services. Reprinted with permission.

What's more, the federal agency charged with enforcing gun laws is the ATF—the very institution whose agents LaPierre once labeled "jackbooted government thugs." Indeed, NRA muscle has helped decrease the size of the ATF relative to other government agencies and to the number of firearms in the country. In 1973, for instance, the Drug Enforcement Agency (DEA) and the ATF had about the same number of employees and the same amount of money; by 1998 the DEA's budget and staff were nearly three times the ATF's.

NRA Hyprocrisy

[In] January [2000], Clinton unveiled the National Gun Enforcement Initiative, which would earmark $280 million in the 2001 budget for 500 new ATF agents and more than 1,000 new federal, state, and local prosecutors. But the NRA has been notably silent about the effort. And with good reason. LaPierre's talk of enforcement is hot air. What he really wants—and what the NRA has always wanted—is for the government to leave gun owners alone.

But it won't. Columbine changed everything, and even staunchly pro-gun Republicans like J.C. Watts have started jumping ship. Worse, so are some of the gun companies. Smith & Wesson, the nation's largest handgun manufacturer, has agreed to install a number of safety features on all its guns in return for an end to lawsuits against the firm. If the NRA had any foresight, it would realize that such settlements are the only way the gun industry can escape an imminent storm of litigation. If the NRA had any political sense, it would applaud Smith & Wesson's decision to install trigger locks on all its guns. But it won't, because underneath its new veneer the NRA is the same organization it has always been. It believes government should keep its nose out of people's guns. That's a principled stand—a principled stand that this magazine and most Americans find utterly loony. Why doesn't Wayne LaPierre say what he really believes? After all, he's going to lose either way.

> "*[Licensing and registration] would make it harder for guns to fall into the hands of children, criminals and the dangerously mentally ill.*"

The Licensing and Registration of Handguns Would Help Reduce Gun Violence

Coalition to Stop Gun Violence

The Coalition to Stop Gun Violence (CSGV) is composed of over forty civic, professional, and religious organizations that advocate a ban on the sale and possession of handguns and assault weapons. The following viewpoint is excerpted from a CSGV brochure promoting the licensing and registration of firearms. The coalition argues that licensing would help reduce gun violence by requiring purchasers to undergo a background check (thus screening out criminals and minors) and to complete a gun safety course. A national firearms registration system, maintains CSGV, would also make it easier for law enforcement to identify the source of illegal weapons used in crimes.

As you read, consider the following questions:

1. What evidence does CSGV offer to show that licensing and registration are effective in reducing gun violence?
2. How would licensing help reduce accidental shootings, in the coalition's view?
3. What is a "straw purchase," according to the authors?

Adapted from *Preventing Gun Violence in America: Licensing and Registration—the Common Sense Solution* (2000), a brochure published by the Coalition to Stop Gun Violence. Reprinted with permission.

E very day, more than 80 Americans—12 of them young people—die from gun violence.

There is a clear, common sense solution.

Licensing and registration.

Why We Need Licensing and Registration

Flint. Columbine. Jonesboro. Grenada Hills. The names and places associated with tragic shootings are all-too familiar. America leads the industrialized world in children killed by guns, in teenagers who take their own or others' lives with firearms, and in handgun injuries and deaths. Twelve children—the number murdered at Columbine—die from gunshot wounds every day in America. Yet, in most parts of our country, there is no system of licensing to ensure that gun owners are responsible and qualified, and no system of registration to track illegal guns.

- America has more guns than adults. Guns are routinely sold through classified ads, over the Internet, or at gun shows—no background checks, no questions asked.
- Nearly two out of three children in grades 6–12 say they could "get a gun if they wanted." Thirty-five percent believe it would take them less than an hour.
- Nearly 40 percent of American households have a gun, yet gun owners aren't even required to know the basics of safe handling or storage.

Where are the laws that should protect us?

- Most existing gun laws do little to limit gun sales or distribution. Even laws that make it illegal to give a gun to a criminal are unenforceable, because there is no national system to register handguns, track their movement into illegal markets, or hold accountable people who sell or use weapons in a criminal or negligent manner.
- Some states have weak gun laws that sometimes contradict tougher laws in other states. Moreover, some state laws place a burden on law-abiding gun owners, but do little to stop criminal trafficking from states with weak gun laws to states with strong laws.
- Despite shooting after shooting, the gun lobby consistently blocks common-sense gun law reform, such as a sensible, enforceable, and Constitutional system of licensing and registration.

Licensing and Registration: How It Works

Handgun licensing and registration is common sense legal reform. In the same way that we license drivers and register cars, this approach would license gun owners (to ensure that they follow basic safety precautions), and register guns (to reduce the chances of illegal sale). Nearly three out of four Americans favor such measures.

Licensing and registration would not take guns from law-abiding citizens. It would require that people who buy guns receive basic safety training. And it would make it harder for guns to fall into the hands of children, criminals and people who are dangerously mentally ill.

What Licensing and Registration:

Would Do	Wouldn't Do
Prevent criminals and children from buying guns	Take guns from law-abiding adults
Ensure that gun owners have had basic training on safe use and storage	Violate the Constitution
Help track guns that are sold or used in a crime	Affect hunting rifles or shotguns
Require gun purchasers to pay a small fee and spend a few hours getting a gun license	Cost taxpayers more than we already pay in the costs of gun violence
Make individuals responsible if their guns are used or sold criminally or negligently	Replace the need for responsible behavior by gun owners

The Coalition to Stop Gun Violence, "Preventing Gun Violence in America: Licensing and Registration—The Common Sense Solution," CSGV brochure, 2000, p. 14.

How effective is licensing and registration? Virtually every other industrialized nation in the world has adopted some form of licensing and registration, with positive results. In all of those countries, rates of gun deaths and murders are far lower than in the U.S. In fact, firearms kill nearly twelve times as many children in America than in twenty-five other industrialized nations combined.

Licensing Gun Owners: Ensuring Basic Safety

Licensing would require gun purchasers to:

- Complete a basic safety course
- Undergo a check to ensure that they have not been convicted of a violent crime or been declared mentally ill by the courts
- Provide a photo and thumbprint, and pay a small fee
- Be licensed locally and renew the license periodically

Many people think we already have licensing and registration. But in most parts of the country, these basic safety precautions do not exist.

Today, without licensing, most Americans are not even required to know the basics of gun safety before purchasing a weapon. That lack of knowledge shows in gun death statistics: a family member is three times more likely to be killed in a home with a gun than in a home that has no firearm.

Licensing wouldn't prevent every gun accident. But it would reduce accidental shootings and deaths by requiring that gun owners are trained in the basics of safe gun handling, including storing guns unloaded and locked where children can't get them.

Licensing would also prevent the sale of guns to those who should not have them. Currently, gun buyers are not required to undergo a background check if they purchase a gun from an unlicensed dealer at a gun show, an exemption under the so-called "gun show loophole." But licensing would require background checks for all gun buyers to ensure that guns do not fall into the hands of children, criminals, and the mentally disturbed.

Licensing wouldn't interfere with law-abiding adults. But it would help keep guns out of the hands of minors, violent criminals and the dangerously mentally ill by requiring that everyone who buys a gun have a license and pass a background check.

Registering Guns: Enabling Law Enforcement

Registration would require that anyone selling a gun:

- Fill out a form with the gun's serial number
- Check to make sure the gun buyer is licensed

- Give a copy of the registration to the gun buyer and send another to law enforcement authorities

Gun owners would renew their gun registration periodically, and when the gun is re-sold.

Registration would help promote responsibility among gun owners in the same way that car owners are made responsible for their cars—by creating a record of ownership and a requirement that gun owners transfer weapons only to other licensed owners. Currently, some disreputable people buy guns legally, in what is known as a "straw purchase," and then sell the weapons under the table to criminals and children. Other people may lend, sell or give guns to friends, who in turn sell or give them to people who shouldn't have them.

While registration would create minimal inconvenience for those who buy and sell guns legally, it would be a major step toward tracing and stopping the illegal sale of guns to criminals and children. Registration would also give law enforcement a new way to identify the source of illegal weapons that are used criminally or negligently.

"Unfortunately for gun control advocates, there is not a single academic study concluding that background checks reduce violent crime."

Gun Licensing and Registration Leads to Increased Crime, Lost Lives

John R. Lott Jr.

John R. Lott Jr. is a senior research scholar at Yale University Law School and the author of *More Guns, Less Crime*. The following viewpoint is adapted from an article Lott wrote for the *Los Angeles Times*, in which he argues against the institution of a gun licensing and registration system in California. Lott maintains that background checks and waiting periods, such as those mandated by the federal Brady Law, have failed to reduce violent crime. Moreover, Lott contends that licensing and registration hurt law-abiding citizens by making it harder for them to obtain a handgun for self-defense. As of 2000, California law required a 10-day waiting period on all gun purchases but did not require individuals to obtain a permit in order to purchase a firearm.

As you read, consider the following questions:
1. Why have handgun registration laws failed to help the police track illegal weapons, in Lott's view?
2. According to the author, why are waiting periods for handgun purchases associated with higher rates of rape?
3. What is Lott's opinion of the training that gun purchasers must receive under California's proposed licensing system?

Reprinted, by permission of the author, from John R. Lott Jr., "Gun Licensing and Registration Leads to Increased Crime, Lost Lives," *Los Angeles Times*, August 23, 2000.

W ho could possibly oppose licensing handgun owners? Requiring training for potential gun owners both in a classroom and at a firing range before they are allowed to buy a gun seems obvious. Licensing, especially when eventually coupled with registration, will supposedly also help identify criminals and prevent them from getting guns.

Yet, as usual with guns, the debate over licensing mentions just the possible benefits while ignoring the real costs to people's safety. If the California Senate passes licensing, it will not only cost Californians hundreds of millions of dollars annually, but, more important, it will increase violent crime.

Theory vs. Reality

In theory, if a gun is left at the scene of the crime, licensing and registration will allow a gun to be traced back to its owner. But, amazingly, despite police spending tens of thousands of man hours administering these laws in Hawaii (the one state with both rules), as well as in big urban areas with similar laws, such as Chicago and Washington, D.C., there is not even a single case where the laws have been instrumental in identifying someone who has committed a crime.

The reason is simple. First, criminals very rarely leave their guns at the scene of the crime. Would-be criminals also virtually never get licenses or register their weapons.

So what of the oft-stated claim that licensing will somehow allow even more comprehensive background checks and thus keep criminals from getting guns in the first place?

Unfortunately for gun control advocates, there is not a single academic study concluding that background checks reduce violent crime.

The Failure of the Brady Law

The *Journal of the American Medical Association* published an article [in August 2000] showing that the Brady law [which instituted mandatory background checks and waiting periods for handgun purchases,] produced no reduction in homicides or suicides. Other, more comprehensive research actually found that the waiting period in the Brady law slightly increased rape rates.

The Clinton administration keeps issuing press releases

boasting that violent crime rates have fallen since 1994, when the Brady law was adopted. Yet violent crime started falling in 1991. The Brady law did not apply to 18 states, but after 1994 their violent crime fell as quickly as other states.

While still asserting that the law "must have some effect," U.S. Attorney. General Janet Reno was reduced to saying, "It might just take longer to measure it."

Registration Is the First Step Toward Confiscation

Perhaps only one other word in the English language so boils [gun owners'] blood as the word "registration," and that word is "confiscation." Gun owners fiercely believe those words are ominously related. . . .

American gun owners know their fears about licensing and registration are hardly unfounded, because they are familiar with the sorry story of gun control in Great Britain. . . .

After passage of the Firearms Act of 1920, Britons suddenly could possess pistols and rifles only if they proved they had "good reason" for receiving a police permit. Then, in 1936, the British police began adding a permit requirement requiring that the guns be stored securely.

As the public grew accustomed to the idea of guns being licensed, it became possible to begin to enforce the licensing requirements with greater and greater stringency. By enforcing the Firearms Act with moderation, at first, and then with gradually increasing severity, the British government acclimated British gun owners to higher and higher levels of control. . . .

Today, in Great Britain, handguns are totally banned. . . .

Those who believe in their Second Amendment birthright will fight mightily to prevent this nation from becoming, like Great Britain, a place where the rights of gun owners are slowly strangled to death because too many people trusted politicians who did not trust them.

National Rifle Association Institute for Legislative Action, "Licensing and Registration," April 9, 2000.

The reason why the Brady law does not affect criminals is simple. It is the law-abiding citizens, not the criminals, who obey the laws. For example, the waiting-period provision in the law prevented law-abiding women who were stalked or threatened from quickly obtaining a gun for self-defense.

Waiting Periods and Licensing Harm Law-Abiding Citizens

There are still other problems with the law that the state Legislature is considering. When added to the current state waiting period, the processing time for a license will delay access to a gun by a month. While even short waiting periods increase rape rates, waiting periods longer than 10 days make it difficult for law-abiding citizens to obtain guns to protect themselves and increase all categories of violent crime.

The hundreds of dollars it will take to pay for the license and the up-to-eight-hour training course, as well as the many arcane reasons for losing a license, will reduce gun ownership by law-abiding people.

Since no other state has such restrictive rules for simply owning a gun, it is difficult to know how much gun ownership will decline, but similar rules for obtaining concealed handgun permits reduce the number of permits issued by 60%. The reduction in permits increased violent crime.

It is already illegal for criminals to go around carrying guns. Making it difficult for law-abiding citizens to even own guns in their own homes is not going to make them safer from the criminals.

Part of the proposed "training" appears better classified as indoctrination, making gun owners memorize grossly exaggerated fears of the risks of owning a gun. It will also be the poor who bear the brunt of these costs and who will be priced out of gun ownership. They are also most vulnerable to crime and benefit the most from being able to protect themselves.

With all the new gun laws already scheduled to go into effect after the November [2000] elections, why don't legislators simply require that California homeowners put out a sign stating: "This home is a gun-free zone"? Legislators could lead by example and start with their own homes.

"The gun industry conducts itself without regard for public safety precisely because it bears none of the costs of that conduct."

Gun Manufacturers Should Be Held Responsible for Gun Violence

Dennis Henigan

Dennis Henigan is director of the Center to Prevent Handgun Violence's Legal Action Project, which helps represent victims of gun violence in suing gun manufacturers. He argues in the following viewpoint that gun manufacturers have failed to take reasonable steps to make their products safer and to keep them out of the hands of criminals. For example, he notes, gun makers have failed to implement trigger locks on their guns that would prevent children from firing them. He believes that holding gun makers accountable in court will force them to take the steps necessary to make guns safer and ensure that they are used responsibly. Moreover, Henigan contends that the monetary costs of gun violence amount to billions in health care and other expenses, and gun manufacturers are partly responsible for those costs.

As you read, consider the following questions:

1. What analogy does the author use to show that a product can be functional but still defective in its design?
2. What is the primary purpose of lawsuits against the gun industry, in Henigan's opinion?

On October 30, 1998, New Orleans became the first city to sue gun makers. Mayor Marc Morial, with the assistance of the Legal Action Project of the Center to Prevent Handgun Violence, has filed a lawsuit against the industry for designing and marketing handguns that lack basic safety features which would prevent shootings by children, teenagers and other unauthorized users. New Orleans seeks to hold the industry accountable for the cost of police, emergency and health-care services that the city pays for due to gun injuries and deaths that would be prevented if gun manufacturers were more responsible in the design of their products.

Since October 30, four other cities—Chicago; Miami-Dade County, Florida; Bridgeport, Connecticut; and Atlanta—have filed lawsuits, and more are sure to follow. While some of these lawsuits follow New Orleans', citing the industry's inexcusable failure to make its products safer, others—particularly Chicago's—focus on the industry's negligent distribution and marketing practices that contribute to a massive illegal gun market.

Although the gun industry claims these lawsuits have no legal merit, it seeks to prevent the courts from deciding the matter. Its longtime front group, the National Rifle Association, or NRA, is pushing for special legislative protection to ensure that judges and juries never hear these cases. A bill which creates immunity from liability exclusively for the gun industry has been enacted in Georgia. A Florida bill would make the mayor of Miami-Dade County a felon for continuing his lawsuit. Other state legislatures are considering similar bills.

Not content to stop there, Georgia Republican Representative Bob Barr, a board member of the NRA, has introduced a bill that would limit lawsuits against the industry by local governments and private citizens. Like the state bills, Barr's bill is a patent attempt to intimidate mayors and others who seek to hold the gun industry accountable for its unnecessarily dangerous products and irresponsible marketing practices.

Three False Claims from the Gun Lobby

What possibly could justify legislative action to block these lawsuits? The gun lobby's arguments reveal a remarkable ignorance of basic principles of American tort law. First, the lobby's spokespeople have argued that gun manufacturers cannot be liable unless their products don't work. According to this argument, only the gun owner whose gun doesn't shoot straight can sue a gun manufacturer. This simply is not true. According to long-accepted principles of product-liability law, a product can be defective in design regardless of whether it malfunctions.

The Ford Motor Co., for example, was liable for fires caused by the placement of its Pinto fuel tank. Even though the fuel tank did not cause the car to malfunction, the placement of the tank created an unreasonable risk that passengers would be incinerated following a collision. Similarly, the failure of gun manufacturers to install safety devices to prevent gun accidents makes guns unreasonably dangerous even if they reliably shoot bullets.

Second, the industry also claims that it cannot be liable because its products are legal. This argument confuses criminal liability, which applies only to illegal conduct, with civil liability, which does not. Most of civil tort law concerns the liability of parties whose actions, though they may be legal, nevertheless are irresponsible and expose others to unreasonable risk of harm. Ford's placement of the Pinto gas tank did not violate any statute, but it created a significant hazard for which Ford was liable.

Moreover, people (and companies) whose conduct violated no law can be held liable for increasing the risk that someone else will act illegally. In 1997, the Florida Supreme Court ruled unanimously that Kmart was liable for selling a rifle to an intoxicated buyer who then shot his girlfriend. Kmart's sale of the gun violated no statute but was so irresponsible that the company was held answerable for the harm caused. Saying that an industry's practices violated no statutes is no defense.

Third, the gun industry also confidently asserts that it cannot be liable when its products are misused by others. If we adhered to this principle generally, we never would have held auto manufacturers liable for selling cars without seat belts and other safety features because most car accidents are caused by driver error.

Guns Should Be Safer

The law wisely imposes a duty on manufacturers to do what they can to reduce the risk of foreseeable injury, even when the wrongful conduct of another is a more direct cause of the harm. The Ohio Supreme Court held that the maker of a disposable lighter may be liable for failing to use feasible means to protect against misuse by children. The court wrote: " A product may be found defective in design where the manufacturer fails to incorporate feasible safety features to prevent harm caused by foreseeable human error." That is precisely the basis for the New Orleans lawsuit: Because the gun industry is well aware that many gun owners make the mistake of leaving guns accessible to children who then misuse them, it should be liable for its failure to use feasible safety systems to prevent this foreseeable, and tragic, misuse of its products. And, as Kmart learned, gun sellers can be liable even when the misuse is criminal.

Holding companies liable for increasing the risk of injury from misuse does not shift the blame away from other culpable parties. It makes all parties who contributed to the harm responsible for their conduct.

The law should punish the reckless driver but not immunize the automaker who could have made the car safer. The law should punish the criminal who uses the gun, but it should not immunize an industry if it fails to take reasonable steps to ensure that criminals cannot misuse the gun. And we are not talking simply about the criminal use of guns. The gun industry is shockingly indifferent to the suicides and unintentional shootings that could be averted if they included basic safety features which would prevent children from using them. When the industry markets guns with so little trigger resistance that a 2-year-old can fire them, why should the blame rest only on the toddler and on the parents who made the gun accessible? Gun manufacturers have the capability to prevent these tragedies from happening. Why should they escape all accountability for failing to do so?

The Role of Litigation

The gun lobby insists that these lawsuits are an improper use of the courts to resolve issues that should be decided by state legislatures. If we want to change the way guns are designed and sold, this argument goes, then such changes should be made by legislatures, not courts. If this argument justifies blocking lawsuits against the gun industry, then it would apply to other industries as well. Yet, the courts did not dismiss the liability lawsuits against Ford on the grounds that the only remedy for victims of exploding Pintos was to seek greater safety regulation of autos from Congress.

This argument is simply disingenuous. The gun industry hardly would support greater regulation imposed by Congress. The industry always has resisted any kind of reform.

Smith & Wesson Agrees to Pursue Smart Gun Technology

On one side have been gun manufacturers, on the other, gun control groups. For decades, it has seemed a polarized, intractable universe—seemingly impervious to the dark procession of gun tragedies on the nightly news.

There may be a third way, essentially based on technology. Its premise is that so-called smart-gun design—manufacturing firearms so that they can only be fired by their owners—can fundamentally change the culture of guns in this country. . . .

That third way is emerging as a result of the federal government-negotiated agreement signed Friday [March 17, 2000,] by the nation's largest handgun manufacturer, Smith & Wesson. . . .

The agreement provides for Smith & Wesson within the next 60 days to begin selling guns with external trigger locking devices; within the next 12 months to design handguns so they cannot be "readily operated" by a child younger than 6; and within 36 months to include "authorized user technology," such as fingerprint activation, in all new firearms models, except certain curios and collector types.

Smith & Wesson is working on two different technologies. In one, the user punches a combination into a keypad. The other uses a fingerprint scanner. . . . The company has spent $5 million on research and has applied for a $3 million government grant.

"Nothing exists today that works," said [Smith & Wesson spokesman Ken] Jorgensen. "We're a minimum of two to three years down the road from anything workable."

Lorraine Adams, *Washington Post*, March 19, 2000.

One purpose of product-liability law is to encourage manufacturers to increase product safety. This is particularly compelling in the case of firearms. Guns, unlike any other consumer product, are exempt from regulation by the Consumer Product Safety Commission. Having used its lobbying clout to protect itself from safety standards, the gun industry now seeks to shield itself from accountability to those injured by its conduct.

The industry's argument of last resort is that the lawsuits are nothing more than greedy lawyers seeking to extort legal fees by threatening a legitimate industry. This argument mimics the response of every industry under legal attack for selling unreasonably dangerous products. It essentially amounts to a strategy of changing the subject. Finding it difficult to defend its conduct, the gun industry makes an issue of the lawyers attacking it.

Of course, the lawyers for the cities will receive contingency fees (a percentage of any award) only if these lawsuits are successful. In contrast, the defense lawyers for the gun industry, who are paid hundreds of dollars per hour, will be paid regardless of whether the industry is vindicated.

The Gun Industry Must Be Held Accountable

The gun industry is a relatively small one that inflicts huge costs on society. Annual sales estimates run anywhere from $1.7 billion to $9 billion. Meanwhile, direct and indirect costs of gun violence amount to more than $23 billion a year, most of which is borne by taxpayers. Given that much of these costs are the result of shootings the industry could prevent, the industry's irresponsibility effectively is being subsidized by taxpayers. Why should this subsidy be allowed to continue?

The gun industry conducts itself without regard for public safety precisely because it bears none of the costs of that conduct. Although it would be entirely fair to shift those costs, the primary purpose of these lawsuits is not to recover damages but to change the way the industry does business.

The mayors who already have filed lawsuits and those who are considering filing are not going to be intimidated by the legislation proposed by Barr. It is not these lawsuits which are frivolous, but his legislation, which grants exclusive immunity to gun manufacturers and denies these mayors and private citizens the fundamental right to be heard in a court of law.

The gun industry has a choice: It can continue business as usual, but only if it pays its fair share of the cost, or it can take the necessary and feasible steps to reduce the misuse of its products by children and criminals. For creating this dilemma for the gun industry, the mayors should be praised, not condemned.

"Gun issues are complex. Should we really leave them to be decided by grasping trial lawyers, grandstanding city attorneys, and activist judges?"

Gun Manufacturers Should Not Be Held Responsible for Gun Violence

Jeremy Rabkin

Jeremy Rabkin, a professor of government at Cornell University, argues in the following viewpoint that lawsuits that blame gun manufacturers for gun violence are frivolous, abusive, and likely to be ineffective in reducing gun violence. Rabkin asserts that the problem of gun violence is not serious enough to warrant such lawsuits and that the social benefits of firearms must be weighed against their harms. Rabkin concludes that, given the complexity of gun control issues, they are best decided by lawmakers, not lawyers. He supports state-level, rather than federal, gun controls, so that different states can experiment with different approaches to reducing gun violence.

As you read, consider the following questions:

1. By the end of 1998, according to Rabkin, what percent of American mayors were considering filing lawsuits against gun manufacturers?
2. How are guns different from tobacco, in the author's view?
3. In Rabkin's opinion, what is the proper way for the government to tell gun makers that it wants tighter restrictions on sales?

Excerpted from Jeremy Rabkin, "Beware the Attack Lawyers," *The American Spectator*, June 1999. © The American Spectator.

After a month of inconclusive bombing against Serbia, [in April 1999] major news organizations turned, almost with relief, to a story they could really illuminate—the high school murder rampage in Littleton, Colorado. It was horrible, and here, and endless numbers of local folks were willing to go on camera to talk about it. So network anchors relocated to Colorado and a grieving nation had the solace of round-the-clock media analysis.

Feel-Good Lawsuits

But what to do about this domestic atrocity? Politicians offered the usual sanctimonious speeches, but therapeutic bombing was not an available option. Instead, the nation seems to be falling back on . . . feel-good lawsuits.

Certainly, the lawyers are ready. The *Washington Post* interviewed a "plaintiffs' lawyer" filled with curiosity about the teenage perpetrators: "I'd like to know where they got these weapons and where this fascination with Hitler came from. There's a possible Internet angle and every time Hollywood makes a movie in which 150 get killed, I think we get closer to a level of responsibility that is compensable." Apparently a lot of other lawyers thought there was "compensable responsibility" by somebody, somewhere: Parents of the slain victims said that lawyers started calling them the week of the funerals.

The idea of holding gun manufacturers liable already has considerable momentum. Early in 1998, Philadelphia Mayor Ed Rendell announced his city would sue major gun manufacturers to recover city expenses for treating gunshot victims. The strained theory behind the suit was that gun manufacturers were responsible for these shootings, even though Philadelphia has severe controls on gun sales, because the gun makers sold a lot of guns in suburbs and surrounding areas, without taking precautions to prevent the guns from ending up in the hands of violent criminals.

Chicago launched a similar suit soon after. By the end of 1998, the U.S. Conference of Mayors reported, 70 percent of American mayors (in cities over 30,000) were "considering" filing parallel suits. And a private lawsuit has already given hope to the mayors.

Activist Courts

In *Hamilton v. Accu-Tek*, victims (or relatives of victims) of shootings in Brooklyn claimed compensation from gun manufacturers for negligently allowing their products into the wrong hands. The presiding federal judge, Jack Weinstein of the Eastern District in New York, had previously presided over innovative "mass tort" cases in which he pioneered the notion that manufacturers could be held liable for their market share, even in the absence of any direct link between a particular firm and injury. [In] February [1999], he guided a divided jury to a similar outcome, after instructing jurors that they could go after gun manufacturers based on their general pattern of sales control, without having to establish a direct link with the perpetrators of the actual shootings. The gun manufacturers are, of course, appealing.

Those who applaud such ventures acknowledge that they amount to activist policy-making by courts—and applaud that, too. New York's new senator, Charles Schumer, has long advocated federal legislation to impose stricter liability on gun manufacturers. Now he is pleased that courts have acted where Congress failed to act: "The courts are a last resort, but we're getting to a point where we need a last resort. It's analogous to *Brown v. Board of Ed.*, where legislators were afraid to do certain things."

The more commonly cited analogy, however, is with class action suits against tobacco companies, where enterprising trial lawyers, allied with state attorneys general, finally pushed the tobacco companies to negotiate a settlement agreement reaching tens of billions of dollars. But tobacco does result in hundreds of thousands of deaths each year, while its social benefits are at least disputable. Guns are different.

First, despite the sensational coverage given to particular episodes, we are not experiencing an epidemic of gun violence. The murder rate has fallen by 30 percent [since 1994]. Most violent crimes—71 percent, according to a 1996 survey—do not involve guns at all. And only 0.2 percent of injuries from violence (according to a survey of hospital admissions) were caused by guns. Meanwhile, twice as many children (14 and younger) died from bicycle accidents as from guns in 1997, and four times as many from drowning.

The Social Benefits of Guns

More importantly, the harm done by guns must be set against the benefits. A recent paper by H. Sterling Burnett, published by the National Center for Policy Analysis, does just that. Despite accidents and criminal abuse, he shows, guns provide net social benefits. A number of reputable studies estimate that there are about 2.5 million episodes a year of "defensive gun use." Most of the time this involves little more than scaring off an attacker by showing the gun. But in some 3,000 cases a year criminals are killed by citizens acting in self-defense—which is three times more often than by police.

Yes, there are accidents and there are shoot-outs in which the party acting in self-defense ends up dead. But your odds improve if you have a gun to use in self-defense: Women facing violent assault were two-and-a-half times more likely to suffer serious injury if they had no firearm compared with those who did. The 22 states that now allow citizens to carry concealed weapons have seen a decline in violent crime.

Sowing the Seeds for Backlash

In their suits against gun manufacturers, the cities . . . further [weaken] the already battered notion of individual accountability upon which our democratic culture depends. . . . Is the next step a class-action suit seeking huge money damages from car manufacturers because of the costs of drunken-driving deaths and joyriding by underage car thieves? . . . .

Lasting policy victories are won in the political arena, not the legal one. When crusaders rely too heavily on the courts—the least democratic branch of government—they inevitably skimp on building public support for their causes, thus sowing the seeds for backlash.

New Republic, March 1, 1999.

Some new controls could perhaps help prevent guns from getting into the wrong hands. But with more than 200 million guns already out there, we shouldn't expect dramatic results. Strict drug laws do not now prevent kids from getting drugs when they are determined to get them. Unlike narcotics, moreover, guns have real value for honest citizens—most of all in helping honest citizens to face the criminals that police can't adequately control (or disarm).

At a minimum, gun issues are complex. Should we really leave them to be decided by grasping trial lawyers, grandstanding city attorneys, and activist judges? . . .

Here are two modest suggestions for finding a way through these thickets. They make sense on policy grounds. They are also, I believe, what the Constitution prescribes.

The first is federalism. There is no reason why gun controls or culture controls should be uniform nationwide. Let different states experiment and let's see how different approaches in response to differing local majorities work. The whole country may have shared Colorado's grief over the Littleton shootings, but it doesn't have to share Colorado's response.

There is a serious argument that the First Amendment should be applied more rigorously to national polices than to state and local policies. As Justice Robert Jackson emphasized and Justice Rehnquist has also noted, the First Amendment begins with the words, "Congress shall make no law. . . . " The Second Amendment, too, might be more indulgent of state than federal controls, since it invokes the importance of state militias in its preamble.

Legislation, Not Litigation

My second suggestion is due process. Policy-making through massive class action claims is abusive, given that defendants had no basis to expect they could be held liable for conduct that's now being challenged. If we want gun dealers to impose tighter restrictions on sales, or movie distributors and Internet sites to restrict access to violent imagery, we ought to tell them so in advance. We have a traditional constitutional mechanism for doing so. It's called legislation.

Hollywood studios and Internet providers alike hate the idea of separate laws in each state. Too bad. They should be even more concerned about class action claims let loose in a capricious national lottery. Compared with class action litigation, the legislative process offers some hope that competing risks and concerns can be held in some reasonable balance, reflecting the opinions of the broader public.

It may turn out that the most useful state efforts don't involve controlling outsiders but improving local schools. Those who think young people are drawn to violence from spiritual emptiness ought to favor voucher programs that make it easier for parents to send children to religious schools. Even public schools might do more to maintain discipline, making it less likely they'll continue as organizing forums for new "trenchcoat mafias" [the name of an antisocial group that the Columbine High School killers purportedly belonged to].

Unleashing attack lawyers is just another form of instant gratification, hitting back blindly when we don't know what else to do. We have a Constitution precisely to restrain such impulses. These days, the Constitution seems not to apply in foreign affairs. But we can still try to respect its wisdom at home.

*"You don't necessarily have to back the
National Rifle Association's political goals
to applaud . . . gun safety training."*

Gun Safety Education Can Help Reduce Gun Violence

Patrick McShea

In the following viewpoint, Patrick McShea describes his experience at a gun safety course at a sportsmen's club in Pennsylvania. He writes that he was impressed with the class's emphasis on education rather than the politics of gun control. McShea notes that in his state, gun safety classes are mandatory for first-time hunters, and he advocates strengthening the laws on mandatory gun safety education. Whether the law mandates gun safety education or not, he concludes, the volunteers who provide such training should be applauded. McShea works for the division of education at the Carnegie Museum of Natural History.

As you read, consider the following questions:

1. What, according to McShea, were the goals of the Hunter-Trapper Education Course that he took?
2. How many hours of hunter-trapper education courses does Pennsylvania law mandate as contrasted with German law, according to McShea?

Reprinted, by permission of the author, from Patrick McShea, "They Give Hunting a Good, Safe Name," *Pittsburgh Post-Gazette*, October 25, 2000, page A-23.

You don't necessarily have to back the National Rifle Association's political goals to applaud the gun safety training conducted by local hunting clubs. My premise is based upon recent experiences in a two-day Hunter-Trapper Education Course at the Logans Ferry Sportsmen's Club in Plum, Pennsylvania.

As I took a seat among 60 classmates in a crowded meeting room for the program's opening session, my attention was drawn to a large NRA poster that bore a message equating gun control efforts with the loss of civil liberties. Eleven hours of instruction loomed ahead, and owing to the poster's prominent position on the back wall, I assumed gun control opposition would be a recurrent theme.

An Emphasis on Education, Not Politics

I could not have been more mistaken. For eight hours on that bright autumn Sunday, and for three more on the following Monday evening, seven volunteer instructors worked tirelessly to shape the opinions and influence the future behavior of an audience that consisted largely of sixth-, seventh- and eighth-grade boys. The team's efforts, however, were exclusively geared to promote the safe handling of firearms, establish standards for ethical conduct afield, and encourage the development of a group mind set that demands high standards of one's hunting companions.

The tone was set early with personal testimony from lead instructor Mike Papinchak about how both shared and solitary hunting experiences had immeasurably enriched his life. He confessed that 20 years in pursuit of large and small game included isolated instances when he retreated from fields, hollows and woodlots after witnessing unsafe behavior on the part of other hunters, and connected his presence at the front of the class to a desire to continue hunting for years to come. "I won't stay in the woods with unsafe hunters, so I'm here today with a lot of helpers to start you all on the road to becoming safe hunters."

Examples of unsafe practices, bad habits, reckless behaviors, ill-advised decisions and even illegal acts were provided through a slide show, but not before the class received some direct instruction about the fundamentals of firearms safety.

Papinchak used an array of shotguns and rifles to explain the name and function of the weapons' components along with the range and destructive power of the ammunition each was designed to fire. Then he startled a front-row student with an abrupt question.

"Would you take this gun from me if I offered it to you?" A mumbled "No" earned a booming "Very good," followed by an even louder "Why?" that was directed to every member of the class.

Gun Safety Education Laws Are Justified

Enforced regulation of laws, written or otherwise, lets people know that irresponsible behavior will not be tolerated. Automobiles haven't been banned to prevent auto accidents; instead, traffic laws are more aggressively enforced. To regulate hunting, a mandated condition for obtaining a license is to pass better education and safety courses. In these and most other activities requiring licenses, a responsible society willingly accepts logical and practical regulation when its value is recognized and unilaterally enforced.

Bart Kendrick, *Gun News Digest*, Summer 1997.

When several class members volunteered that they didn't know if the weapon was loaded, Papinchak praised their critical thinking, then asked everyone to reconsider the situation under slightly different circumstances. "What if I showed you that the safety was on?" Silence and quizzical looks reigned for a few long seconds until the veteran hunter supplied the proper response and the reasoning behind it.

"The answer is still 'no.' Safeties are mechanical devices and mechanical devices can fail." Using vocabulary he defined for the group only minutes earlier he stated, and then slowly repeated for emphasis, the course's initial major point. "Confirming a gun is unloaded by opening the action is the only way to accept a firearm."

Thinking Critically About Firearm Safety

The exchange typified all that followed. At every stage of the course, instructors prodded their pupils to think critically, oftentimes while they were on their feet outside. Small group sessions during the afternoon included closely supervised target shooting on the club's rifle range as well as a guided walk-through course on a wooded portion of the 145-acre property. Here course participants carefully carried dummy guns with pine plank stocks and barrels of galvanized pipe as they negotiated a half-mile-long winding path that crossed fences, fallen trees and a steep-banked stream.

"Shoot or no-shoot?" instructor guides called out periodically whenever a strategically placed, three-dimensional target drew the attention of the advancing column. A simple "yes" or "no" without an explanation of the attendant reasoning was considered an insufficient answer, and wavering decisions invariably generated a repetition of the question along with the statement of another fundamental point. "Shoot or no-shoot. If you're at all unsure, it's always a no-shoot situation."

In Pennsylvania, hunter-trapper education courses have been mandatory for all first-time hunters since 1982. A 10-hour minimum for the programs was established in 1986. According to Game Commission records, current annual participation in the training programs runs between 35,000 and 40,000 individuals.

"All those people aren't all automatically recruited into the ranks of hunters, of course," explains commission spokesman Bruce Whitman, "But we feel strongly that the courses can also be valuable to people who choose not to hunt, particularly in the case of a young person who comes from a home where people hunt, or a home with firearms in it."

An Invaluable Service

Towards the end of *Buck Fever*, Mike Sajna's masterful 1990 book about deer hunting in Pennsylvania, the author ties the future of hunting to the pastime's public image and laments the fact that training requirements in this country do not more closely match the 100-hour commitment German hunters mandate for themselves: "Every year I realize once more how much I do not know or appreciate about deer hunting, a world I might have understood better sooner if American hunters were required to undergo more formal training before entering the field."

The published thoughts of the recently deceased *Pittsburgh Post-Gazette* outdoors writer will doubtless continue to frame a good argument for years to come. But I think Sajna would heartily agree that, under the current system, dedicated volunteers like those at Logans Ferry Sportsmen's Club provide an invaluable service.

"If firearm related injuries and death are to decrease, citizen involvement must increase."

Community Organizations Can Help Reduce Gun Violence

Join Together

Join Together is a project of the Boston University School of Public Health that serves as a national resource for communities working to reduce substance abuse and gun violence. In the following viewpoint, Join Together discusses how individuals can come together to reduce the levels of violence in their area. The organization describes several communities' success stories in violence prevention and provides tips to individuals on how they can become involved in their own communities.

As you read, consider the following questions:
1. What is the Village Houses program, as described in the viewpoint?
2. According to Join Together, what methods did the Baton Rouge Partnership for the Prevention of Juvenile Gun Violence use to reduce gun violence?
3. Why is it important for individuals to educate themselves about the harms associated with gun violence, according to Join Together?

Excerpted from *How Communities Can Take Action to Prevent Gun Violence* (Summer 1999), a publication of Join Together, a project of the Boston University School of Public Health. Reprinted with permission.

A few facts about gun violence:

- Approximately 150,000 Americans are injured by gunfire every year, requiring some $20 billion in direct medical treatment.
- The annual death toll from gunfire in recent years exceeded 34,000.
- Thirteen kids under the age of 19 are killed by guns every day.
- Compared to other countries, America has significantly more gun violence. In 1996, for instance, handguns were used to murder 30 people in Great Britain, 106 in Canada, 15 in Japan, and an astounding 9,390 in the U.S. In addition, American children are 12 times more likely to die from gun injury than children from all other industrialized nations combined.

Get Involved

So what can you do to bring these numbers down? Work with a broad range of others in your community to devise and implement a strategy aimed at preventing gun violence. Collaborative efforts involving citizens and key leaders have succeeded in reducing gun violence. For instance, a partnership between the police, clergy, parents, youth workers and community groups in Boston developed a strategy that reduced teen gun deaths in that city by more than 80%.

Now is the time to educate elected officials and other decision-makers in your town and state about the high cost of gun violence, both in terms of lives lost and medical expenses incurred. Now is the time to work together with other groups to assess your community's situation and develop an appropriate strategy.

Now is the time to write an op-ed for your local newspaper calling on your state legislators to support and implement new anti-violence legislation. Now is the time to join together and take action.

[In 1998,] the two-county area served by the Central Florida Prevention Coalition [CFPC] lost 17 young people to gunshot wounds and another 17 to drug overdoses. When Kathleen Sager Blackburn, community awareness coordinator for the coalition, looked at the deadly parity in those numbers, they made an impression.

"The thought struck me that the problems are equivalent," she says. "We also know they're interrelated, that there's a direct correlation between the two. That's why we focus on both."

The CFPC, which is located in Orlando and serves Orange and Seminole counties, is an excellent example of a substance-abuse organization that has expanded its reach to address the related problem of gun violence as well.

Two years ago, for instance, CFPC joined forces with another group, the Central Florida Partnership for Nonviolence, as well as the Orlando Police Department, to sponsor a gun buyback program. With the assistance of a funding partner, a company that provided $50 vouchers for each gun turned in, the sponsors bought back 400 firearms in three hours.

The group also sponsors annual Martin Luther King Day "youth memorial" marches, in which participants carry posters of youths who have died, to raise public awareness. "We march in memory of the youths who died untimely deaths due to drugs, guns, and suicide," Blackburn says.

A third project that CFPC has organized with an eye toward easing the threat of gun violence is called the Village Houses program. "Village houses" are designated homes of volunteers in high-risk neighborhoods where children can go after school or on weekends and feel relatively safe in a gun- and drug-free environment. There are currently 20 Village Houses in the CFPC service area. "One of the major problems for many kids," Blackburn says, "is that they don't have a safe place to go after school when both parents are working and drug dealers are on every corner."

Gun Violence and Drug Trafficking

Another locale that has recently begun to expand its interest in gun-violence prevention is Youngstown, Ohio. With a population of about 100,000, Youngstown has drawn attention as a city particularly troubled by gun violence. [In 1998,] the city recorded an astonishing 66 homicides, making it the deadliest city in Ohio and the fourth worst in the nation.

By all accounts, the gun-violence problem in Youngstown is directly related to drug trafficking, as Mayor George M.

McKelvey emphasized in a letter to former President Bill Clinton, heavily publicized in the local press. . . . In the letter, McKelvey asked Clinton to dispatch his drug czar, Gen. Barry R. McCaffery, to Youngstown, to assist the city in finding ways to deal with drug-related violence. "Youngstown is being held hostage by armed criminals terrorizing our city with the gun violence that goes hand-in-hand with their drug trade," McKelvey wrote.

Joining Together to Make a Difference

Recognizing that the loss of over 34,000 lives a year to firearms in the United States is unacceptable, communities from across the country are joining together in an effort to stem the tide of gun-related injuries and deaths. . . .

An increasing number of national and state groups, dedicated to reducing firearm-related injuries and deaths, have emerged over the past several decades in response to this problem. National gun violence prevention groups like the Coalition to Stop Gun Violence, Handgun Control, Inc., the Violence Policy Center, and the HELP Network are:

• lobbying for more responsible gun legislation;

• working to change firearm-related policy;

• building alliances and forming coalitions;

• providing leadership and resources for grassroots organizers;

• conducting valuable gun-related research;

• providing survivors of violence with an opportunity to share their stories and find support; and

• raising awareness about the harms associated with guns through media advocacy, events and public awareness campaigns.

Join Together, "The Response: Joining Together," www.jointogether.org/gv/issues/response/join.

One part of the community's response is based in Youngstown's St. Elizabeth's Hospital. Funded by a three-year grant from the University of Pennsylvania Medical Center and the Joyce Foundation, the hospital trauma center is now a lead agency in studying the problems of drugs and gun violence in Youngstown. Meanwhile, the city is assembling a program funded by a Justice Department grant for the purposes of developing more effective law-enforcement strategies to combat drug-related violence. A third effort is occurring in the Juvenile Justice Center courthouse, where a grant from the Justice Department's Office of Juvenile Justice and Delinquency Prevention is funding a new program to initiate strategies to counteract youth violence.

In Baton Rouge, La., the Baton Rouge Partnership for the Prevention of Juvenile Gun Violence, formed in 1997, grew out of a task force that was formed in 1989 to combat a crack-cocaine epidemic. Aided by a grant from the Office of Juvenile Justice and Delinquency Prevention (OJJDP), the Partnership seeks to reduce gun violence through a variety of methods, including high-intensity monitoring of known multiple gun offenders; universal gun traces; and working closely with the local Bureau of Alcohol, Tobacco and Firearms. But it also includes an educational component that covers training of life skills, school-based programs, and anti-violence clinics. In addition, the partnership works to create summer jobs, cultural and recreational activities for youths, and teen summits.

According to Yvonne Day, project director for the Mayor's Anti-Drug Task Force in Baton Rouge, the results have been noticeable. Since the birth of the Partnership, violent crime among juveniles has declined by 22 percent.

But just as important, Day says, is the fact that the city has built a structure that can move forward. "For the first time in our community," she says, "we have a multi-dimensional community initiative that's not just 'lock 'em up'."...

Take Action

Get Involved: Gun violence is preventable, but if firearm related injuries and deaths are to decrease, citizen involvement must increase. Take action to influence positive change through public policy, outreach and media advocacy initiatives. By doing so, you will join a growing number of people who are working to make their communities safer places to live.

Get Started: It is not uncommon for individuals to feel somewhat overwhelmed and helpless by the problems that occur in their communities. Frequently as a result, people choose not to get involved. But the truth is that everyone can do something to help. Your volunteer support is valuable to grassroots community efforts, and your ideas and opinions are meaningful to your legislators in helping to determine local and national policy. Frequently, legislators or their aides talk about how they feel compelled to vote against sensible gun-related legislation because they receive significantly more phone calls, letters, visits or faxes from pro-gun supporters. If the gun lobby matters, then so do you. Until individuals who are concerned about gun violence become as politically active and outspoken as the pro-gun lobby, lenient gun laws will remain in place.

Another key reason individuals may choose not to be more active in their community is the uncertainty about how to get started or whom to contact. Here are some tips to help to facilitate this process:

- Educate yourself about the harms associated with gun violence in your community. Knowledge is empowering; by learning more about the issue of gun violence you are in a better position to do something about it.
- Assess what is already being done in your community to prevent gun violence. Check with local violence prevention groups, youth and civic groups or law enforcement officials to find out what is being done in your area and who the key contacts are.
- Join a local community group in your area or a national organization that is working to prevent firearm violence and find out how you can help. The directory on Join Together Online at www.jointogether.org/gv lists numerous organizations working to reduce gun violence across the country. You might also try contacting local foundations to see which gun violence prevention initiatives they fund in your community.
- Encourage family, friends, neighbors and co-workers to get involved in issues that affect your community. Involved citizens working together can make a difference!
- Start a project or group addressing the issue of firearm-related violence in your area if you are unable to find one. There are organizational support services available to help you in your planning. Starting a grassroots organization can be a time-consuming and exhausting pro-

cess, however, so it may be best to explore your options with already existing organizations before moving forward with your planning so as not to duplicate efforts.

Work with the Community

Collaborate: It is easier to bring about lasting change when you have the support of a cross section of organizations and people representing your community.

Coalitions, collaboratives or partnerships serve as an effective way to bring different segments of a community together to solve social problems such as gun violence. They connect individuals and groups with current information and resources, including success stories from other communities. As a result, issues can be more effectively addressed than through single agencies working alone.

Faith and religious communities, law enforcement agencies, elected officials, grassroots community groups, health care professionals, peace and social justice organizations, domestic violence prevention groups, survivors, students, schools, media, businesses, academia, child welfare and women's organizations, and professional networks are all natural allies in the fight against gun violence. Expand your base and broaden your gun violence prevention efforts through the following collaborative steps:

Key Steps:
- Begin strategic planning in your community by convening key officials, heads of organizations, and community leaders involved in gun violence prevention work.
- Contact federal, state and local elected officials. Invite them to meet with your coalition and keep them informed of the coalition's activities. Emphasize the importance of collaboration among federal and state agencies, as well as collaboration between each level of government.
- Pool resources with other prevention groups to conduct a gun violence prevention resource assessment within your community. Assess the needs in your community with a survey and focus groups with key organizations such as schools, police, health officials, religious groups and community members.

- Determine the priorities for your community's gun violence prevention strategy after gathering information on resources and needs.
- Evaluate your coalition periodically to determine what organizations and individuals need to be involved. Strength comes from inclusion. Also, periodically measure your results to determine the group's success and to make necessary changes in your strategy.

Strategize: To effectively implement change, you must have a strategy in place. Whether your objective is to influence public policy, change attitudes or raise awareness, it is advantageous to have a clear understanding of how policy, outreach and media can play a major role in helping to achieve your goals.

What You Can Do

Youth: Do you feel frustrated by the level of violence in your school or neighborhood? Do you worry about threats or intimidation from a fellow classmate? Are you feeling pressure to join a local gang? Or are you concerned about a friend who has been feeling suicidal in recent months and who may have access to a gun? Regardless of the circumstances, there are others who have been in your shoes and there are people and resources that can help.

Although you may feel alone with your fear of guns or gun violence in your community, there are other young people who have felt like you do. You can play an important role in helping to ensure that your school and neighborhood is a safe place to be. By joining a violence prevention group, being a peer leader, or participating in a youth service program, you can make a difference in your community. . . .

Parents: Parents are the greatest influence in a child's life. As a parent and as a keen observer of your child's growth and well-being, you are in a unique position to provide a safe, supportive, and nurturing environment for your child.

There is much that you as a parent can do to ensure that your children feel safe within the home and within the wider community. Helping your children understand the dangers of guns and gun violence, teaching them to resolve conflict peacefully and ensuring that, if you have a gun in the home, it is stored safely—are some of the suggested ways to keep your family safe. . . .

Educators and School Administrators: Providing a safe learning environment for students is a common goal among all educators. Accomplishing this goal requires the commitment of communities, businesses, parents and students working together. Whether you have had a student bring a gun to school, intervened in a conflict among students involving a gun, or been on the receiving end of threats or intimation by a student carrying a gun, you are undoubtedly invested in helping to stop the violence.

Educators can have a tremendous impact on their students through activities such as classroom discussions on conflict resolution, implementation of a Safe School Plan, or involvement of students in community-wide activities that help to increase the awareness of dangers related to firearms.

There are numerous curriculum and resource materials as well as programs that have been developed to train teachers on how to implement violence-prevention strategies in their classrooms and schools.

Periodical Bibliography

The following articles have been selected to supplement the diverse views presented in this chapter. Addresses are provided for periodicals not indexed in the *Readers' Guide to Periodical Literature*, the *Alternative Press Index*, the *Social Sciences Index*, or the *Index to Legal Periodicals and Books*.

Sarah Brady and John R. Lott Jr.
"Would New Requirements for Gun Buyers Save Lives?" *Insight on the News*, June 21, 1999.

Fox Butterfield
"May I See Your Gun License, Please?" *New York Times*, January 29, 2000.

Angie Cannon
"The New Smart Guns," *U.S. News & World Report*, January 24, 2000.

Issues and Controversies on File
"Gun Industry Lawsuits," October 15, 1999.

Gary Kleck
"Guns Aren't Ready to Be Smart," *New York Times*, March 11, 2000.

David B. Kopel
"Taking It to the Streets: Treating Guns Like Cars," *Reason*, November 1999.

Newsweek
"Guns in America: What Must Be Done," August 23, 1999.

Walter Olson
"A Smith and Wesson FAQ," *Reason*, June 2000.

Kenneth Smith
"Gun Control That Works: Project Exile in Richmond," *Reader's Digest*, November 1999.

John Michael Snyder
"Firearms Education May Lead to Reducing the Rate of Violent Crime," *Insight on the News*, March 1, 1999.

Susan B. Sorenson
"Regulating Firearms as a Consumer Product," *Science*, November 19, 1999.

For Further Discussion

Chapter 1

1. The Violence Policy Center (VPC) maintains that gun violence is a serious problem, while Dave Kopel argues that gun control advocates often exaggerate the problem. Whose argument do you find more convincing? Might there be truth to both viewpoints? Explain.

2. The VPC emphasizes statistics indicating that over half of all homicides are committed with handguns. In contrast, Dave Kopel points out that 75 percent of murders are committed by people who already have criminal records. Based on this and other contrasts in the two viewpoints, how do you think the two authors would differ in their approaches to reducing gun violence?

3. Barry Glassner argues that gun violence among youth has decreased. Does the Children's Defense Fund acknowledge this point? Does the fact that gun violence is decreasing—among youth or in the general population—make you feel that gun violence is less of a problem or that increased efforts to reduce the problem are unnecessary? Explain.

Chapter 2

1. C. Emory Burton states that "where there are fewer guns, there is less gun violence," while Glen Otero claims that studies have shown that "areas with high gun ownership experienced less crime than comparable areas with lower firearm ownership." What evidence does each author provide to support their claim, and who do you find more convincing?

2. Burton argues that countries with lower levels of gun ownership have lower rates of firearm death. How does Otero respond to this argument? Is he convincing? Why or why not?

3. Based on the viewpoints by Don B. Kates and Douglas Weil, do you think concealed-carry laws increase or decrease levels of gun violence? Explain your answer. In your opinion, should individuals be allowed to carry concealed weapons?

4. Thomas Sowell relies largely on a common-sense argument that guns can be used to protect as well as harm, while Handgun Control Inc. cites a variety of statistics, as well as describes a few instances of accidental shootings, to argue that handguns in the home decrease personal safety. Which approach is more

persuasive, in your opinion? Would you feel safer keeping a gun in the home? Why or why not?

Chapter 3

1. Both Rachana Bhowmik and Stefan B. Tahmassebi discuss the case of *United States v. Miller*. How does Bhowmik summarize the Supreme Court's ruling in that case, and how does this contrast with Tahmassebi's interpretation of the ruling?

2. Does Tahmassebi believe that gun control laws are unconstitutional? Explain your answer using quotes from the viewpoint.

3. Based on the viewpoints by Larry Craig and Michael W. Warfel, do you feel that gun control laws infringe on Americans' Second Amendment rights? Why or why not?

4. Charlton Heston argues that gun ownership is necessary to prevent the government from abusing its power over individual citizens. Do you find this argument convincing? Explain your answer.

Chapter 4

1. Charlton Heston claims that federal gun control laws were not adequately enforced under the Clinton administration, while the editors of the *New Republic* reject that claim and argue that new gun control laws are needed. Do you agree with Heston that the problem of gun violence can be adequately addressed by enforcing existing laws, or do you agree with the *New Republic* that new laws are needed?

2. The Coalition to Stop Gun Violence believes that licensing and registration of firearms would make it harder for criminals to obtain guns and easier for law enforcement to identify people who illegally sell guns to criminals. How does John R. Lott Jr. respond to this reasoning? Do you find his counterarguments convincing? Why or why not?

3. List the reasons Dennis Henigan offers in support of lawsuits against the gun industry, as well as the points Jeremy Rabkin makes against such lawsuits. Of the several arguments each author makes, which two do you find most persuasive?

Organizations to Contact

The editors have compiled the following list of organizations concerned with the issues debated in this book. The descriptions are derived from materials provided by the organizations. All have publications or information available for interested readers. The list was compiled on the date of publication of the present volume; the information provided here may change. Be aware that many organizations take several weeks or longer to respond to inquiries, so allow as much time as possible.

American Civil Liberties Union (ACLU)
132 W. 43rd St., New York, NY 10036
(212) 944-9800 • fax: (212) 869-9065
website: www.aclu.org

The ACLU champions the rights set forth in the Declaration of Independence and the U.S. Constitution. The ACLU interprets the Second Amendment as a guarantee for states to form militias, not as a guarantee of the individual right to own and bear firearms. Consequently, the organization believes that gun control is constitutional and, since guns are dangerous, it is necessary. The ACLU publishes the semiannual *Civil Liberties* in addition to policy statements and reports.

Cato Institute
1000 Massachusetts Ave. NW, Washington, DC 20001
(202) 842-0200 • fax: (202) 842-3490
website: www.cato.org

The Cato Institute is a libertarian public-policy research foundation. It evaluates government policies and offers reform proposals and commentary on its website. Its publications include the Cato Policy Analysis series of reports, which have covered topics such as "Fighting Back: Crime, Self-Defense, and the Right to Carry a Handgun," and "Trust the People: The Case Against Gun Control." It also publishes the magazine *Regulation*, the *Cato Policy Report*, and books such as *The Samurai, The Mountie, and The Cowboy: Should America Adopt the Gun Controls of Other Democracies?*

Center to Prevent Handgun Violence
1250 Eye Street NW, Suite 802, Washington, DC 20005
(202) 289-7319
websites: www.cphv.org • www.gunlawsuits.com

The center is the legal action, research, and education affiliate of Handgun Control Inc. The center's Legal Action Project provides free legal representation for victims in lawsuits against reckless gun manufacturers, dealers, and owners. The center's Straight Talk About Risks (STAR) program is a violence prevention program designed to help youth develop victim prevention skills and to rehearse behaviors needed to manage conflicts without violence or guns. Its websites provide fact sheets and updates on pending gun lawsuits.

Citizens Committee for the Right to Keep and Bear Arms
12500 NE Tenth Pl., Bellevue, WA 98005
(206) 454-4911 • fax: (206) 451-3959
website: www.ccrkba.org

The committee believes that the U.S. Constitution's Second Amendment guarantees and protects the right of individual Americans to own guns. It works to educate the public concerning this right and to lobby legislators to prevent the passage of gun-control laws. The committee is affiliated with the Second Amendment Foundation and has more than six hundred thousand members. It publishes several magazines, including *Gun Week*, *Women & Guns*, and *Gun News Digest*.

Coalition to Stop Gun Violence (CSGV)
1000 16th St. NW, Suite 603, Washington, DC 20002
(202) 530-0340 • fax: (202) 530-0331
website: www.csgv.org

The CSGV lobbies at the local, state, and federal levels to ban the sale of handguns to individuals and to institute licensing and registration of all firearms. It also litigates cases against firearms makers. Its publications include various informational sheets on gun violence and the *Annual Citizens' Conference to Stop Gun Violence Briefing Book*, a compendium of gun control fact sheets, arguments, and resources.

Handgun Control, Inc.
1225 Eye St. NW, Suite 1100, Washington, DC 20005
(202) 898-0792 • fax: (202) 371-9615
website: www.handguncontrol.org

A citizens' lobby working for the federal regulation of the manufacture, sale, and civilian possession of handguns and automatic weapons, the organization successfully promoted the passage of the Brady Bill, which mandates a five-day waiting period for the purchase of handguns. The lobby publishes the quarterly newsletter *Progress Report* and the book *Guns Don't Die—People Do* as well as legislative reports and pamphlets.

Independence Institute
14142 Denver West Pkwy., Suite 101, Golden, CO 80401
(303) 279-6536 • fax: (303) 279-4176
website: www.i2i.org

The Independence Institute is a pro–free market think tank that supports gun ownership as both a civil liberty and a constitutional right. Its publications include issue papers opposing gun control, such as "Children and Guns: Sensible Solutions," "'Shall Issue': The New Wave of Concealed Handgun Permit Laws," "Unfair and Unconstitutional: The New Federal Gun Control and Juvenile Crime Proposals," as well as the book *Guns: Who Should Have Them?* Its website also contains articles, fact sheets, and commentary from a variety of sources.

National Crime Prevention Council (NCPC)
1700 K St. NW, 2nd Fl., Washington, DC 20006-3817
(202) 466-6272 • fax: (202) 296-1356
website: www.ncpc.org

NCPC is a branch of the U.S. Department of Justice. Through its programs and educational materials, the council works to teach Americans how to reduce crime and to address its causes. It provides readers with information on gun control and gun violence. NCPC's publications include the newsletter *Catalyst*, which is published ten times a year and the book *Reducing Gun Violence: What Communities Can Do.*

National Rifle Association of America (NRA)
11250 Waples Mill Rd., Fairfax, VA 22030
(703) 267-1000 • fax: (703) 267-3989
website: www.nra.org

With nearly three million members, the NRA is America's largest organization of gun owners. It is also the primary lobbying group for those who oppose gun control laws. The NRA believes that such laws violate the U.S. Constitution and do nothing to reduce crime. In addition to its monthly magazines *America's 1st Freedom, American Rifleman, American Hunter, InSights,* and *Shooting Sports USA,* the NRA publishes numerous books, bibliographies, reports, and pamphlets on gun ownership, gun safety, and gun control.

Second Amendment Foundation
12500 NE Tenth Pl., Bellevue, WA 98005
(206) 454-7012 • fax: (206) 451-3959
website: www.saf.org

The foundation is dedicated to informing Americans about their Second Amendment right to keep and bear firearms. It believes that gun-control laws violate this right. The foundation publishes numerous books, including *The Amazing Vanishing Second Amendment*, *The Best Defense: True Stories Of Intended Victims Who Defended Themselves with a Firearm*, and *CCW: Carrying Concealed Weapons*. The complete text of the book *How to Defend Your Gun Rights* is available on its website.

U.S. Department of Justice
Office of Justice Programs
P.O. Box 6000, Rockville, MD 20850
(800) 732-3277
websites: http://ojjdp.ncjrs.org/gun/index.html • www.ojp.usdoj.gov/bjs/welcome.html

The Department of Justice protects citizens by maintaining effective law enforcement, crime prevention, crime detection, and prosecution and rehabilitation of offenders. Through its Office of Justice Programs, the department operates the National Institute of Justice, the Office of Juvenile Justice and Delinquency Prevention, and the Bureau of Justice Statistics. Its publications include fact sheets, research packets, bibliographies, and the semiannual journal *Juvenile Justice*.

Violence Policy Center
2000 P St. NW, Suite 200, Washington, DC 20036
(202) 822-8200 • fax: (202) 822-8202
website: www.vpc.org

The center is an educational foundation that conducts research on firearms violence. It works to educate the public concerning the dangers of guns and supports gun-control measures. The center's publications include the report *Handgun Licensing and Registration: What it Can and Cannot Do*, *GUNLAND USA: A State-by-State Ranking of Gun Shows, Gun Retailers, Machine Guns, and Gun Manufacturers*, and *Guns for Felons: How the NRA Works to Rearm Criminals*.

Bibliography of Books

John M. Bruce and
Clyde Wilcox

The Changing Politics of Gun Control. Lanham,
MD: Rowman & Littlefield, 1998.

Philip J. Cook and
Jens Ludwig

Gun Violence: The Real Costs. New York: Oxford
University Press, 2000.

Vic Cox

Guns, Violence, and Teens. Springfield, NJ:
Enslow, 1997.

Jennifer Croft

*Everything You Need to Know About Guns in the
Home*. New York: Rosen, 2000.

Tom Diaz

*Making a Killing: The Business of Guns in
America*. New York: New Press, 1999.

Jan E. Dizard,
Robert Merril Muth,
and Stephen P. Andrews
Jr., eds.

Guns in America: A Reader. New York
University Press, 1999.

Wilbur Edel

*Gun Control: Threat to Liberty or Defense Against
Anarchy?* Westport, CT: Praeger, 1995.

George A. Gellert

*Confronting Violence: Answers to Questions About
the Epidemic Destroying America's Homes and
Communities*. Boulder, CO: Westview Press,
1997.

James Gilligan

Violence: Our Deadly Epidemic and Its Causes.
New York: G.P. Putnam, 1996.

Don B. Kates Jr. and
Gary Kleck

*The Great American Gun Debate: Essays on
Firearms and Violence*. San Francisco: Pacific
Research Institute for Public Policy, 1997.

Gary Kleck

Targeting Guns: Firearms and Their Control. New
York: de Gruyter, 1997.

Wayne R. LaPierre

Guns, Crime, and Freedom. New York: Harper-
Perennial, 1995.

John R. Lott Jr.

*More Guns, Less Crime: Understanding Crime and
Gun-Control Laws*. University of Chicago Press,
1998.

Maryann Miller

Working Together Against Gun Violence. New
York: Rosen, 1997.

James M. Murray

Fifty Things You Can Do About Guns. San Francisco: Robert D. Reed, 1994.

Ted Schwarz

*Kids and Guns: The History, the Present, the Dan-
gers, and the Remedies*. New York: Franklin
Watts, 1999.

Joseph F. Sheley

*In the Line of Fire: Youth, Guns, and Violence in
Urban America*. New York: de Gruyter, 1995.

Peter Squires   *Gun Culture or Gun Control: Firearms, Violence, and Society*. New York: Routledge, 2000.

Josh Sugarmann   *Every Handgun Is Aimed at You: The Case for Banning Handguns*. New York: New Press, 2001.

William Weir   *A Well-Regulated Militia: The Battle Over Gun Control*. North Haven, CT: Archon, 1997.

Index